To Byron from

Bob

The Beauty of Clocks

by
Michael Pearson

Produced by
Ted Smart & David Gibbon

First published in Great Britain 1979 by Colour Library
International Ltd.
Colour separations by La Cromolito, Milan, Italy.
Printed and bound by RIEUSSET, Barcelona, Spain.
Published by Crescent Books, a division of Crown
Publishers Inc.
All rights reserved.
Library of Congress Catalogue Card No. 78-59735
CRESCENT 1978

Contents

Introduction

The astonishing growth in the interest in antiques in general and clocks in particular during the past ten years is due as much to the media and the number of publications and television programmes on the subject, as to the desire in most people to get away from the throw-away plastic society in which we live. The more advanced our society becomes, the more we try to recapture the past. Collecting antiques is just one further way of doing this. There is a fascination in handling articles that were made many years ago by craftsmen who would have no place in today's mass-production world. For some reason, clocks seem to evoke more interest than most antiques, possibly because they are not only beautiful to look at but also serve a useful purpose.

Whilst any book on clocks has to contain a certain amount of technical information, only enough has been included to provide a background to the main theme which is the general history of clockmaking. For anyone who is more interested in the technical side of the subject, there are many eminent volumes available and a list of required reading is given in the Bibliography at the end of this book. What I have attempted to do is interest the general reader in the world of clocks, and show by the many fine colour plates just how beautiful these examples of past craftsmanship really are. Inevitably, some of the clocks illustrated are in the great museums, but the vast majority of those specially photographed for this book have been on the market until very recently. In view of the fact that so much of our antique heritage is being exported (and clocks are no exception), it is hoped that the plates used throughout this book will provide a valuable guide to what is fast being lost abroad, and be a source of pleasure through the years to come, both to the general reader and the avid collector.

Plate 1 *A superb silver-mounted three train musical bracket clock by Charles Gretton in Fleet Street. Of special interest are the fine hands and the beautifully pierced silver basket top incorporating the Coat of Arms of the 2nd Earl of Radnor for whom this clock was made circa 1690.*

Plate 2 *Early English lantern clock with alarm by William Selwood circa 1650.*

Plate 3 *A mid-nineteenth century French ormolu clock on a gilded stand.*

Plate 4 Left *Part of the interior of Kent Clocks Services workshop.*

1. Early history until 1500 A.D.

From the very beginning of man's existence on this planet, his life has been governed by time, which in its turn is controlled by the movement of the earth in relation to the sun and the Solar System. Many of the early civilizations worshipped the sun, and for thousands of years man has attempted to probe the mysteries of space. Astronomy is one of the oldest sciences known to us and by observing the apparent movements of the sun and moon, men arrived at a system whereby the year is divided into days and months. It is now widely thought that many of the relics left by early man, such as stone circles of which Stonehenge is probably the best example, are in fact astronomical clocks.

It is difficult for us to understand just how important a part the sun played in primitive societies when virtually everybody was engaged in agriculture and man's working life coincided with the hours of daylight. Very little could be done after dark owing to the poor quality of artificial illumination which was limited to open fires and rush candles. Even as late as Stuart times, in the seventeenth century, the hours that people kept were quite different from our own. There are many references by the famous diarist, Samuel Pepys, in his fascinating account of life in seventeenth century London: of his rising at 4 o'clock, going to his office at the Admiralty, eating at 11 o'clock in the morning, having dinner at five in the evening and going to bed at nine, a daily routine which is quite alien to us living in the twentieth century!

It was only natural, therefore, that the sundial was the first time-keeping device to be developed by the early civilisations of the Middle East and Egypt, as the shadow cast by an upright object was the most obvious way of observing the position of the sun and the passing of time.

The Greeks subsequently developed a more sophisticated version, using the shadow of a pointer on a marked plate, and this became the standard type of sundial and was used throughout Western Europe for many centuries. It can, in fact, still be purchased today although, in the majority of cases, they are only used as garden ornaments. Whilst the sundial is a fairly simple device, it is very accurate, and because of the inaccuracy of the early mechanical clocks, sundials were still used to regulate them. In fact, the sundial was still being used to regulate clocks until the advent of the electrical clock in the late nineteenth century, when it became possible to transmit a time signal by cable over fairly long distances.

Obviously the main disadvantage of the sundial is that it is useless at night and during cloudy weather, and to counteract this the Egyptians and the Chinese developed the water-clock (clepsydra), which measures the dripping of water through a small hole. Many elaborate and sophisticated clepsydra were devised, some utilising automata and wheels in the mechanism hundreds of years before the advent of true mechanical clocks. The two other methods which were in common use were the burning of candles marked with the hours, and the hour-glass, which measured the passage of sand between two glass-bulbs joined by a narrow funnel. This method uses the same principle as the water-clock and was still in use in the Navy until late in the eighteenth century.

Before the fourteenth century, day and night were divided into two twelve hour periods, but as the length of the solar day is not constant, owing to the fact that the earth's orbit around the sun is an ellipse rather than a circle, it meant that on only four days a year did solar time and mean time (the 24 hours of the average day) coincide. These days are known as Equinoxes, and occur on the 16th April, 14th June, 1st September and 25th December. There is, in fact, a difference of up to

Plate 5 *A Saxon gold and silver pocket sundial, circa 850 A.D.*

sixteen minutes between the two, depending on the time of year. As society became more advanced it was necessary to have a more accurate method of time-keeping and at some time in the fourteenth century, the modern method of dividing a day into 24 equal hours came into general use, with the exception of Italy which persisted with the old method until late in the Middle Ages.

During the early Middle Ages, i.e. the tenth to fourteenth centuries, the church was the dominant factor in most people's lives. It was also the centre of learning and the originator of the majority of the technical and cultural advances which took place in Europe at that time. Owing to the need of the monasteries and the church to regulate their daily routine, a more sophisticated means of time-keeping became necessary, and they were probably the first to develop a mechanical clock, primarily to call people to services. In the monasteries it was not uncommon for up to seven services a day to be held. Pocket sundials had been used for this purpose and Canterbury Cathedral possesses a beautifully made gold and silver example which marks the time of three services by the shadow cast by a gold pin which is inserted into one of the three holes on the face of the dial (Plate 5).

This is the earliest known device in this country for telling the time, dating from circa 850 A.D. and is thought to have belonged to a Saxon king.

2. Early mechanical clocks

Plate 6 *A German circular gilt table clock, circa 1600.*

It is believed that the earliest mechanical clock was set up in a church in Milan, Italy, in 1335. Italy at that time was the birthplace of the Renaissance, which was to set off an astonishing increase and interest in learning, bringing tremendous cultural, artistic and technical advances, and this movement was ultimately to spread throughout the rest of Europe by the end of the century. We are particularly fortunate in that two of the oldest mechanical clocks in existence are in this country, one at Salisbury Cathedral, which has been restored and can be seen in full working order, and is thought to date from 1386. The other, from Wells Cathedral in Somerset, is now in the Science Museum in London.

These early clocks had both dials and striking mechanism actuated by Jacks in the shape of human figures, thus enabling the time to be told by day and night. All the early clocks were mounted on very heavy wooden frames in church towers and very few survive intact. One of the most well-known examples is the Rye Church clock which has the quarters struck by Jacks in the form of cherubs. However, this clock is thought to date from much later, probably the sixteenth century.

All mechanical clocks are weight-driven and derive their power from a rope coiled round a drum, the release of which drives the wheels; the device by which the speed of release is regulated is known as an escapement. The earliest form of this was the verge which was controlled by a foliot, a horizontal bar with adjustable weights at either end (fig. 1). By moving the weights along the bar it was possible to increase or decrease the foliot swing and thus regulate the clock. At this time all these so-called turret clocks were set up in public places and used the foliot method of escapement. During the latter part of the fifteenth century, a demand arose for a much smaller clock which would be suitable for domestic use. As a result, the chamber clock evolved, which was a smaller version of the turret clock in every way except that it utilised the balance wheel method of escapement (fig. 2).

The weight-driven mechanism was fitted in an open iron frame and was hung on the wall so that the weights which drove the wheels could hang freely. It is generally believed that all the chamber clocks made at this time were manufactured on the continent and it has to be admitted that during this period the standard of metal work on the continent was much higher than in England. One has only to visit the Victoria and Albert Museum in London to view the magnificent examples of ironwork, particularly locks, made by the German craftsmen of the day to appreciate this fact.

Obviously, these early clocks had the one great

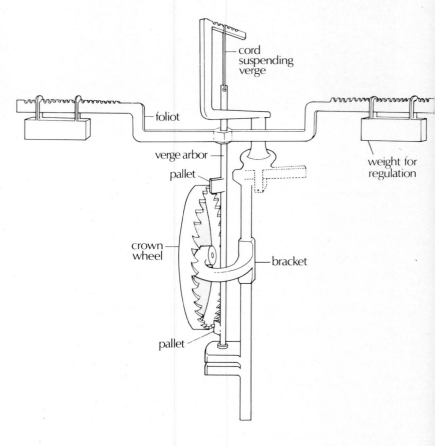

Figure 1 *Verge escapement.*

disadvantage that they were not portable, and at some time in the late fifteenth century spring-driven table clocks and clock-watches which could be hung from a person's belt came into use. These clocks utilized a coil spring to provide the power to drive the mechanism. However, the early springs were very unreliable and difficult to produce. There was also the inherent problem that a coiled spring exerts more power when fully wound than when it has nearly run down. To

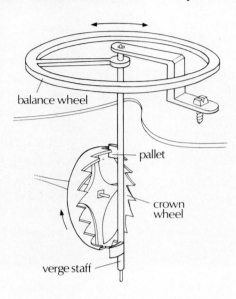

Figure 2 *Balance wheel escapement.*

Plate 8 Bottom left *A French table clock in gilt-brass, engraved with scenes of The Four Seasons, adapted from designs of the months by Etienne Delaune with its original embossed leather case. This clock was made by Felix Loubet who was working in Paris during the second half of the sixteenth century.*

Plate 7 Top right *A late sixteenth century German gilt-brass clock with engraved and cast decoration.*

Plate 9 Bottom right *A gilt drum table clock, circa 1620.*

counteract this, the German clockmakers invented the device known as the Stackfeed, (fig. 3). However, this proved to be very inefficient and was not used to any great extent by the rest of Europe who employed the fusee, a much simpler and more effective method of controlling the release of the coiled spring. Although no-one knows who invented this ingenious device, it had been known of for some time. There is a sketch in existence by Leonado da Vinci of a fusee movement, but there is no evidence to suggest that he was responsible for its invention.

Most of these early table clocks were in the shape of round drums and had the dials placed on top. Unlike the earlier chamber clocks, the mechanism was

mounted between two flat metal plates rather than in an open frame. Not only were they very expensive and invariably owned only by members of the aristocracy, but also most unreliable. They used the balance wheel escapement which is difficult to regulate and in many cases variations in time-keeping of up to fifteen minutes was possible. However, it must be appreciated that except for the sundial this was still the most accurate method of time-keeping yet devised.

Many fine examples of this type of clock are in existence, some of the cases having very elaborate decorations in brass and silver-gilt. Almost without exception, these clocks were made on the continent in the Low Countries, France and Germany.

At this time English clockmaking was in its infancy

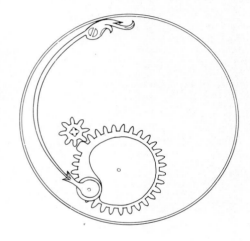

Figure 3 *Detail of the Stackfreed, a device used by the early German makers to equalize the force of a fully wound coiled spring. The small roller at the end of a spring presses against the shaped cam. The mainspring arbor has a pinion which comes up against the stop on the wheel thus ensuring that only a few turns of the spring are made, at which time the forces exerted are almost equal. As the mainspring unwinds the friction caused by the small roller decreases as the shaped cam revolves.*

Plate 10 Above Left *A French travelling clock made of engraved gilt-brass, with alarm work in a stamped and gilt-leather case, dating from the late sixteenth century. Right: A south German miniature clock in gilt, brass and silver with translucent enamel panels. Late sixteenth century.*

Plate 11 Bottom *(From left to right)*
German table clock in gilt-brass with silver dial. Dated 1581. A German table clock made of engraved gilt-brass, signed by Michael Wagner of Breslau. Circa 1675. German table clock in gilt-brass, with a silver dial, signed by B. Firstenfelder of Friedberg.

Plate 12 Opposite page *A German copper-gilt clock. Early seventeenth century.*

and was largely in the control of the Blacksmith's Company who, whilst being skilled craftsmen in metal, could not compare with the intricate skills possessed by their continental counterparts who were mostly locksmiths and used to dealing with much finer work. However, during the time of the Tudors, England was enjoying a greater period of prosperity than she had ever known, and inspired by the Renaissance, the English court had become a prime centre of learning and scientific interest under the influence of Henry VIII. Whilst he is mostly remembered today, purely for his ill-famed collection of wives and sundry bloodthirsty exploits, it is often forgotten that in his early years he was considered one of the leading scholars of the day, showing an intense interest in the new discoveries which were being made at that time in all fields. The inevitable result of this new prosperity was an increase in the standard of life for the upper classes in particular, and a demand for the luxury goods which were finding their way into the country in increasing quantities from the mainland of Europe.

In addition, the religious persecution on the continent drove many Protestants to leave the Low Countries and France to find refuge in England which

Figure 4 *The fusee.*

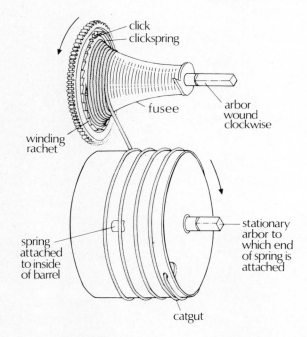

Plate 13 Opposite page *Detail of superbly-engraved dial of a late sixteenth century south German clock in copper-gilt.*

Plate 14 Above *A German gilt-bronze clock of the early seventeenth century.*

Plate 15 Below *(Left to right) A French table clock made of gilt-brass. The sides are engraved with the parable of The Good Samaritan and it is signed by B. Pichart who was working in Paris in 1640.*
Another French gilt-brass of the late sixteenth century, from Aix-en-Provence. The clock sides are set with rock-crystal.

by this time had broken with the Roman Catholic Church after Henry's feud with the Pope over his divorce from Katherine of Aragon, and the establishment of the English Church after the dissolution of the monasteries. These refugees included large numbers of craftsmen of all trades who thus brought their superior skills to the benefit of this country. This accounts for the fact that many of the early clockmakers had French-sounding names, and amongst their descendants can be numbered some of the best makers of the late seventeenth and early eighteenth century. A fine example of an early musical clock by Nicholas Vallin, a Flemish refugee working in

London at the close of the sixteenth century, is shown in Plate 18.

One of the very few English spring-driven table clocks to survive is shown in Plate 16. This clock is signed by David Ramsay who was clockmaker to James I and it can be seen in the Victoria and Albert Museum. It has very fine engraving and pierced work to the case and may well be French in origin as it is known that Ramsay worked in France.

It must be remembered that these early table clocks were very intricate pieces of work, with cases of brass and silver-gilt often superbly carved and engraved. As a result they were very expensive and were only available to the most wealthy section of the population, i.e. members of the Court, and a few merchants in the city of London. However, towards the end of the sixteenth century, a peculiarly English form of clock appeared and has come to be known as the Lantern clock. It was made to hang on the wall and employed a four post construction being descended from the earlier chamber clocks. As a general rule these clocks were much cruder than the continental spring-driven varieties and as a result were cheaper and within the purchase range of the rapidly-growing merchant class. It must be pointed out however, that many examples were made in silver and covered with fine engraving, and were obviously intended for use in the great houses of the time, perhaps in the domestic quarters. Although the majority of the clocks of this type to be seen today are of brass and steel construction, they still have finely engraved dials. With very few exceptions they had one hand and ran for 30 hours only, having to be wound every day by pulling on an endless rope or chain from which the single weight which drove the mechanism was suspended. These early lantern clocks were made in great numbers during the sixteenth and seventeenth centuries and although

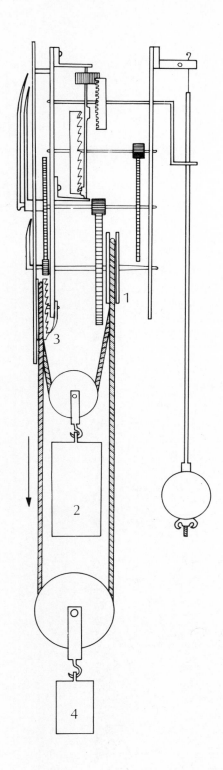

they soon became unfashionable in London, following the introduction of bracket and longcase clocks, they continued to be made throughout the eighteenth century in country districts. However, examples do exist made by some of the most famous craftsmen, e.g. George Graham, and these were probably utilised in the servants' quarters of the great houses, whilst small examples contained within wooden cases were used as travelling alarm clocks.

As can be seen from four clocks illustrated in Plates 2, 19, 21, and 22 Lantern Clocks were usually fitted with a subsidiary alarm dial which is the innermost ring on the face of the clock. Details of the internal construction of the clock by Thomas Wheeler is shown in Plate 20.

Plate 18 Below *The earliest-known musical clock with carillon striking. Made by Nicolas Vallin of London in 1598. This clock has a verge escapement with balance wheel.*

Figure 5 *Detail of Huygen's timepiece controlled by a pendulum and driven by a single weight suspended on an endless rope. Published in 1658.*

Plate 16 Left *One of the very few English table clocks in existence. This clock is signed by David Ramsay, who was clockmaker to James I. The case is beautifully engraved and pierced and it is possible that it came from France as Ramsay is known to have worked in Paris before 1610. He was appointed the first Master of the Clockmaker's Company on its incorporation in 1632.*

Plate 19 Above *Brass Lantern clock with alarm work, dating from the third quarter of the seventeenth century. Made by Thomas Wheeler of London who was apprenticed in 1647, appointed Master of the Clockmaker's Company in 1684 and died in 1694. A particular point of interest is the pierced frets using intertwined dolphins, the commonest form of fret found on Lantern clocks.*

Plate 20 Below *Detail of the internal mechanism of the Thomas Wheeler clock.*

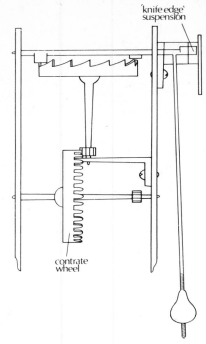

Figure 6 *Drawing of verge escapement with bob pendulum.*

Plate 22 Opposite *A very fine Lantern clock by Ahasuerus Fromanteel, made circa 1670. This clock is very unusual in that it has minute markings on the chapter ring and has two hands. Most Lantern clocks had hour hands only. Also note the bob pendulum in front of the dial. This was quite common with Dutch clocks, but was rarely seen in England.*

Plate 21 Above *An early English Lantern clock with alarm and verge escapement with balance. The alarm mechanism is mounted on the exterior of the back-plate. Made by William Bowyer who was working in London from 1626-1647 and was one of the founder members of the Clockmaker's Company.*

3. The founding of the Clockmakers' Company and the years of English supremacy

During the early years of clockmaking in England the majority of the craftsmen were foreigners and up until the appointment of Bartholomew Newsam in 1590, even the post of Royal Clockmaker was invariably given to a foreign maker. Randolph Bull was the next Englishman to hold the appointment at a salary of 12 pence a day and he was replaced on the accession of James I by a Scot, David Ramsay, who had trained in France, and kept the post for the next fifty years, amassing a considerable fortune in the process, more from his aristocratic connections than his skill as a clockmaker. During this period the industry was largely in the hands of and under the control of the foreign immigrant craftsmen and their dominance was the cause of growing resentment amongst the increasing

Plate 23 Below *One of the earliest English longcase clocks, made by Ahasuerus Fromanteel in London, circa 1660. Note the very fine early dial with a narrow chapter ring and cherub spandrels with superbly carved and filed hands. The movement has a verge escapement with bob pendulum, subsidiary date ring and bolt and shutter maintaining power. The case of oak is veneered with ebony and decorated with gilt-bronze mounts.*

Plate 24 Right *Another longcase by Ahasuerus Fromanteel in ebony, circa 1675.*

numbers of English-born makers. A group of them banded together to petition the King to form a Clockmakers' Company separate from the Blacksmiths' who had controlled the industry hitherto. Their aims were to regulate the methods of working and conditions of employment and to restrict the growing numbers of foreigners who were taking away their livelihood. At the second attempt a Charter of Incorporation was granted on the 22nd August, 1631. This Charter laid down the basic rules by which the industry was governed for the next hundred and fifty years, with the main emphasis on conditions of work and the standards required in order to maintain a high quality of workmanship.

During these early years of the Company there were a host of squabbles and internal quarrels and anybody interested in learning more about this very complicated period is recommended to read Brian Loomes' excellent account in his volume: "Country Clocks and Their London Origins". This book also gives a great deal of

new information concerning the Fromanteel family who are now thought to have introduced the pendulum to England, thus ushering in the golden age of clockmaking and the beginning of English supremacy in the craft which was to last for over a hundred years.

One of the great problems of these early clocks using the foliot or balance-wheel methods of escapement was that they were very unreliable timekeepers and could rarely keep time without a fifteen minute variation each day. However, during the 1650's, an event occurred which was to revolutionise clockmaking: the invention of the pendulum, which made really accurate timekeeping possible for the first time. The famous astronomer Galileo is thought to have discovered the isochronous property of the pendulum in 1581, i.e. that a pendulum has a regular period of swing from side to side, and the speed of the swing is regulated by the length of the pendulum. This can easily be adjusted by raising or lowering the pendulum bob, thus making it go faster or slower. In 1657 the Dutch scientist Christian Huygens Van Zulicham first applied the principle to clockwork (see Fig 5) and gave the right to use his invention to a clockmaker from the Hague called Salomon Coster. At this time John Fromanteel, an apprentice and relative of Ahasuerus Fromanteel was working with Coster and a direct result of this co-operation was that in October 1658 Ahasuerus, the most famous member of this family, advertised a new form of clock regulated by a pendulum which gave far greater accuracy than any time-keeper known previously, when used with the verge form of escapement. As a result of more detailed research which has been carried out on the family in the past few years, the Fromanteels can now be elevated to the most prominent position in the history of clockmaking in England. Members of the family were often in trouble with the Clockmakers' Guild and one of the reasons for this is thought to have been their membership of the Anabaptist religious sect which was opposed to the Restoration of the Monarchy under Charles II and is probably the reason why Ahasuerus Fromanteel was never given the official acclaim which his work and skills demand.

After the restoration of Charles II to the throne of England, in 1660 the country eagerly turned its back on the austere Puritan way of life and living standards improved tremendously, with a consequent increase in the demand for luxury goods. As a result, vast quantities of tapestries, silks and furniture were imported and the change in architectural and furniture design caused both as a result of the Dutch influence,

Plate 25 Left *An early floral marquetry longcase clock by John Ebsworth, London, circa 1675. This clock has very unusual astronomical work on the dial. Note the 'Barley-Twist' columns on the hood which were very common on clocks of the late seventeenth century, and also the finely-carved cresting. This is rarely seen as the crests were usually carved of lime wood which is very susceptible to woodworm, and very few have survived.*

The Progressive Development of the English Longcase Clock Dial

1665

1665

1670

1680

1690

1690

1690

1695

1700

1700

1705

1705

1710

1715

1715

1720

1725

1770   1770   1780

1785   1800   1810

1800   1810   1820

brought back by the Court from Holland and the need to rebuild London after the Great Fire in 1666, created a huge market for household goods. The new designs were more suited to the elegant interiors of the brick and stone buildings which were beginning to take the place of the old wooden houses; these had been mostly furnished with heavy oak which was now replaced by a more graceful style in walnut and other lighter woods. The new type of clock in its wooden case which was predominantly architectural in design was an admirable addition to these new styled interiors.

Charles II was actively interested in scientific advancement and incorporated the Royal Society in 1662 which included among its members the leading scientists and thinkers of the age: such men as Isaac Newton, Robert Hooke and Christopher Wren. This society was the cradle and inspiration for almost all of the significant advancement and inventions that took place in science, mathematics and medicine during the late seventeenth and early eighteenth centuries. It is also no coincidence that the pre-eminence of England and Holland in clockmaking had much to do with their supremacy as the two major seapowers of the time. The Greenwich Observatory was founded in 1675 to investigate more accurate methods of time-keeping with a particular emphasis on finding longitude, which is essential to accurate navigation. However, this particular problem was not solved until the middle of the eighteenth century. The next major development was the introduction of the long pendulum used in conjunction with the anchor escapement (fig.7). This is thought to have been invented by the mathemetician, Robert Hooke, but was first used by a leading London maker, William Clement, around 1675. The use of the long pendulum gave far greater accuracy and it was now possible to make clocks that went for eight days, a month, three months or even a year at one winding.

Although the brass Lantern clock was still being made and continued to be made until the late eighteenth century, the longcase clock now became the more popular style. The advent of the anchor escapement in conjunction with the long pendulum, giving a very narrow pendulum swing, meant that it was now possible to enclose the mechanism inside a

Plate 30 *Three fine marquetry clocks.* **Left** *Longcase of oak, veneered with walnut and olive wood oysters, 8 day movement, by Francis Rainsford of London, circa 1690. The marquetry shows the early Dutch influence.* **Centre** *Fine small longcase clock with 10″ dial, by Jonathon Lowndes of London, circa 1690, only 6′ 3″ high.* **Right** *Late seventeenth century longcase with 11″ square movement, by Christopher Gould of London, an eminent clockmaker. The bird and flower marquetry is set in ebony panels.*

Plate 31 Above *A rare bird and flower all-over marquetry longcase clock with 11″ dial, count wheel strike, pin date adjustment and 6′ long pendulum which beats every 1¼ seconds instead of the usual one second. Note the glass lenticle in the plinth, showing the pendulum bob. The front of the plinth hinges open for pendulum regulation. Made by Benjamin Johnson, circa 1690.*

Plate 32 Right *A superb example of a Dutch marquetry longcase clock. An 8 day movement with alarm work with Dutch quarter striking on two bells of different pitch. Made by Jacob Hasius of Amsterdam who is recorded as working from 1682 until 1725. Compare this clock with the English examples to see the difference in case design.*

wooden case, thus producing a pleasing piece of furniture and protecting the delicate machinery from dust and accidental damage at the same time. However, some of the early longcases still utilised the short bob pendulum with the verge escapement. These clocks were usually narrow in the trunk and quite short, 5′ 6″ or so, architectural in style with a simple panelled case made of ebony or oak veneered with ebony. They were occasionally embellished with gilt mounts but their main purpose was to show the beautifully simple early dials to their best advantage so that nothing detracted from the main object of telling the time. Two very fine examples are shown in Plates 23 and 24.

The dials were made of brass with the centre portion matted with a fine punch, and were fitted with cherub spandrels which were superbly finished by hand and often mercurial gilded. The hands were also carved and filed by hand and then blued in hot sand and oil over a

Plate 33 Above *Two fine examples of the later style of English marquetry, which developed into very intricate designs, commonly called 'Seaweed' marquetry. Both clocks cases are of oak veneered with walnut, and marquetry of various woods. The clock on the* **left** *is by Henry Godfrey of London, and the clock on the* **right** *by Henry Poisson of London. Both circa 1700.*

Plate 34 Right *Superb walnut marquetry clock with arabesque decoration, by Henry Harper of London. This fine clock is in the classic Queen Anne Style and a special note should be made of the fine original carved mouldings and finials. Harper was a noted maker and this clock was probably made circa 1705.*

fire. The separate chapter rings and subsidiary date and seconds ring were silvered and in the finest clocks were often of real silver. The dials of the early longcase clock were mostly 9″, 9½″ or 10″ in diameter and were fitted with a very narrow chapter ring on which were engraved the minutes and half-hour markings. The actual mechanism was mounted between two brass plates held together by pillars which were usually decorated with turned rings and were 4, 5 or 6 in number, depending on the size of the plates. The pillars were secured either by metal pins or brass latches. On many of the clocks produced by the leading makers, much of the steelwork was beautifully carved and finished. When one considers that the internal mechanism was not often seen, it gives an insight into the care and attention to detail and pride in their craft which was shown by the early makers.

One of the regulations of the Clockmakers' Company was that every clock should be signed by its maker and in the early years the signature appeared at the foot of the dial plate, but as the width of the chapter ring increased, it became usual for the name to be engraved at the base of the ring on either side of the number VI.

Unlike the backplates of bracket clocks, longcase movements were almost never engraved, although it was usual for the finest makers, such as Thomas Tompion, to number their clocks either on the backplate or the rear of the dial plate.

Towards the end of the seventeenth century, dial sizes increased to 11″ and 12″ in diameter with an increase in the amount of engraving to the dial and the use of far more ornate hands. There was also a change in the design of the spandrel or corner pieces which were fitted to the dial-plate. These became more elaborate until about the year 1700; the use of a spandrel incorporating two cherubs holding aloft a crown was the commonest type in use. The easiest way of showing the various stages in the development of the clock dial is to look at a number of enlargements of dials which are depicted in their approximate date order. The full progression of dial development from 1670

until 1840 is shown on pages 22, 23, 24 and 25. It must be appreciated that many of the styles overlapped as it would have been uneconomic for a clockmaker to have scrapped his stock of parts merely to cash in on the new fashions and innovations. At this time the new styles all emanated from London and therefore it is to be expected that country clocks will usually show signs of some of the earlier features years after they had been jettisoned by the leading makers in the capital.

Towards the end of the seventeenth century, the early style of longcase clock housed in a very simple, black architectural case, went out of fashion and the walnut case, either plain or decorated with simple inlaid

Plate 36 Above *Detail of the going train of the Finch movement. John Finch was a fine maker, apprenticed in 1668 and appointed Master of the Clockmaker's Company in 1706.*

Plate 35 Left *Typical 11″ five-ringed pillar, 8 day longcase movement, by John Finch of London, circa 1695, showing detail of inside locking plate strike action.*

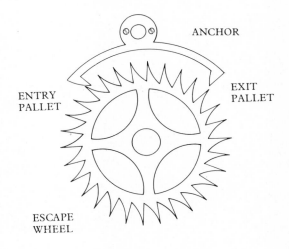

Figure 7 *The 'Anchor' escapement*

boxwood and ebony lines came into favour.

In 1685 Louis XIV revoked the Edict of Nantes and the resultant religious persecution led many thousand of Protestants to seek refuge in England. Amongst this further influx of refugees were many craftsmen, including goldsmiths, clockmakers and cabinet makers, bringing with them much higher standards of design and workmanship, particularly in cabinet making. Marquetry and lacquer work had been popular on the continent for some years and the fashion for decorated

30

Plate 37 Opposite page, left *One of the finest longcase clocks in the British Museum's collection, by Thomas Tompion, who is recognised as the greatest English clockmaker of all time. This clock is of one months' duration and is contained within a very fine oak case, veneered with mulberry wood, and ebony stringing. Clock cases in this wood are very rarely found. Circa 1700.*

Plate 50 Opposite page, right *Another superb longcase clock of the Queen Anne period, from the British Museum's collection, by Tompion's great contemporary, Daniel Quare. The movement is of one year's duration and has a subsidiary calendar and equation dial in the trunk. The long hand of this dial makes one revolution per year, and shows the day and the month. The small hand indicates the equation of time. The small dials are for the days of the week and pendulum regulation. The case is of walnut veneers with very fine gilded brass mounts. Circa 1705.*

furniture immediately swept the country on its arrival and soon overflowed into the clockmaking industry. The early plain ebonized or walnut case was soon superseded by cases decorated with intricate inlays of bird and flower patterned marquetry. In the earliest examples the decoration, usually of tulips and carnations, was laid in panels on an ebony ground. The more expensive clock cases were also sometimes inlaid with ivory or bone. During the next fifteen years the marquetry became more and more ornate, and in some instances the whole case would be covered in floral designs. The Dutch influence in marquetry eventually gave way to a typically English form, using arabesque or seaweed patterns of very intricate design and invariably executed in sycamore on a walnut ground.

These marquetry cased clocks are now the most sought after specimens and command very high prices; examples by the most eminent craftsmen, such as Thomas Tompion, the Knibb brothers, Dan Quare, Joseph Windmills are rarely to be seen and are beyond the reach of all but the wealthiest of collectors. Whilst the cases, and in many instances the dials also, became more and more ornate, certain makers, notably Tompion, probably the most famous maker of all, still preferred to use a simple style of case and dial in order that nothing detracted from the main purpose of telling the time.

Even at this early stage of the development of the clockmaking industry, few clocks were made wholly by one man. The very few styles of spandrel used, for example, suggest that certain craftsmen specialised, producing various parts: dial-plates, hands, wheels etc. and that the majority of the clocks sold were merely put together by the clockmaker or his apprentices.

Plate 39 Top right *Another longcase clock from Tompion's workshop, in ebonized pearwood, veneered on oak. This clock is signed by Tompion and Banger and dates from 1705. Edward Banger was apprenticed to Tompion whose niece, Margaret Kent, he married, and was subsequently taken into partnership. Many fine clocks, both bracket and longcase, survive from this time bearing Tompion and Banger's joint signature.*

Plate 40 Right *A fine burr-walnut clock from the end of the period of the square dial, circa 1710. This clock has an 8 day striking movement with a 12″ dial and is by Joseph Jackeman of London Bridge who is recorded as working from 1682 until 1716.*

Obviously, a certain amount of extra finishing was done to the movement, depending on how much a prospective purchaser was prepared to pay. Cases were also the work of a specialist and were usually of oak, veneered with walnut, laburnum or olive wood oysters; burr elm and mulberry wood veneers were also used. Oak was very rarely, if ever, used by the London makers in its plain form although many fine country examples exist in this medium, and it continued to be used by the country makers until late in the eighteenth century. At the same time that marquetry decoration

arrived in this country, a vogue for lacquer decorations came into favour. This stemmed from the trading activities of both the English and the Dutch East India companies in the Far East, and their importation of lacquered furniture which had been the fashion in China for many years.

With the publication in 1688 of "An illustrated Treatise of Japanning and Varnishing" by Stalker and Parker, it soon became a very popular pastime and much furniture was lacquered at home by the female members of the household. Even fine walnut pieces

Plate 41 Below left *A good quality walnut longcase clock by Joseph Windmills. This clock is an early example of the change from square to break-arch dials. The calendar work in the arch is typical of Windmills. Note the crown and cherub spandrels and dolphin spandrels surrounding the boss in the arch. Circa 1715.*

Centre *The provincial version of the arch-dial longcase. This clock is by Stephen Harris of Tunbridge. The movement has 5 pillars and inside locking plate striking and is of London quality. The case is oak with walnut cross and feather banding to the trunk door and plinth. Circa 1720.*

Right *Another fine quality arch dial London clock by Thomas Cartwright, in a finely-figured walnut veneered case. Note the later mask head spandrels. Thomas Cartwright was watchmaker to Queen Anne and George I.*

Plate 42 Opposite page, left *A very fine year duration walnut longcase, by William Webster of London, circa 1715, another of Thomas Tompion's apprentices who made some fine clocks, many with astronomical work. Note the panel of bevelled Vauxhall glass set into the trunk door. This unusual feature is to be seen on other clocks by this noted maker who was made a warden of the Clockmaker's Company, and died in 1734.*

Plate 43 Right *An example of an early arch-dial clock of 3 month duration, by Thomas Tompion circa 1710, in an ebonized case with gilt mounts. Note the very fine spandrels and the engraving in the arch. It is interesting to note that while most of Tompion's contemporaries made great use of marquetry and lacquer decoration, he preferred plain cases, using beautifully-figured walnut or mulberry wood veneers, or ebonized pearwood veneers on oak, which went out of favour with other London makers before 1690.*

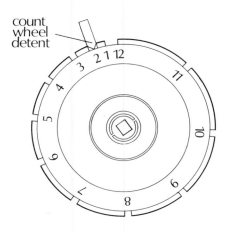

Plate 44 Left *An early example of lacquer decoration, simulating tortoiseshell, by Joseph Knibb, London, circa 1690. A craze for chinoiserie decoration on furniture and clock-cases swept the country with the increasing imports of oriental items by the East Indies Company at the end of the seventeenth century, and the accession to the throne by William III in 1688 with the consequent Dutch influence. Lacquer work had been popular there for many years.*

Figure 8 *Count-wheel method of striking.*

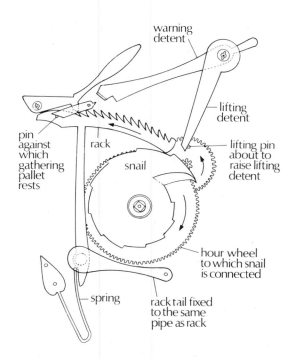

Figure 9 *Detail of rack striking mechanism.*

Plate 45 Far left *A fine example of an early provincial lacquer longcase by John Wimble of Ashford in Kent, circa 1705. The 8 day rack-striking movement has four pillars and repeating work. Note the retention of the convex moulding under the hood, which had been superseded by a concave moulding by London makers by 1700.*

Left *A good lacquer longcase with black and gold decoration, by Thomas Elliot of Greenwich, circa 1710. The movement is of 8 days duration with five ringed pillars and inside locking plate striking. The dial is only 11½" square.*

Plate 46 Above *A very fine red lacquer clock by Thomas Windmills, who succeeded his father Joseph, and was appointed Master of the company in 1719.*

Plate 47 Right *Another superb lacquer longcase with rare blue and silver decoration of very fine quality. This clock is signed Markwick Londini and was probably made by James Markwick the Younger, circa 1725. He was an eminent maker and was Master in 1720.*

were sometimes lacquered over in this fashion. This fashion originated in the Far East and in its correct form utilises the lac or resin obtained from an insect which, when applied to a wooden carcase after numerous coatings, gives a hard, brilliant finish. However, the correct method was very laborious, and owing to climatic conditions, could only be carried out in the East. The Dutch and English lacquerers, therefore developed a quicker method, using coatings of gesso to which was added a basic ground colour. On top of this was drawn the oriental style decoration which was then coloured with silver and gold powders. The most common colours used were red, black and green, although blue, yellow and orange are sometimes to be found. In the later stages the lacquer work degenerated

Plate 48 Opposite page *Three interesting clocks spanning 100 years of clockmaking.*
Left *Walnut longcase with 12″ five pillar rack-striking movement, by Burges of London, circa 1710.*
Centre *Interesting green lacquer longcase by Fry of Kilmersdon, twelve miles east of Bristol. This clock not only shows the phases of the moon, but also indicates the time of high water at Bristol quay. Circa 1740.*
Right *Mahogany longcase clock with 8 day painted dial movement. Circa 1800.*

Plate 51 Above *Two fine mahogany clocks from the collection in the Victoria and Albert Museum. The clock on the* **left** *is a superb provincial example by Richard Peyton of Gloucester, circa 1750. The other clock was made by Mitchell and Mott in New York in typical Sheraton style, circa 1800.*

Plate 49 Top left *Dial and hood of a typical pagoda-top London mahogany longcase clock by William Webster, circa 1760. This style of case was often found with lacquer decoration from 1735 until the 1760's when mahogany became the first choice for clock cases.*

Plate 50 Left *Another mahogany clock of the George I period, of very good proportions and with a finely-figured case. By Alexander Hare, circa 1785.*
The mahogany bracket clock is by the famous maker, John Ellicott, and was made circa 1760. The signature and strike/silent lever are located on the square silvered dial which can be seen when the door is opened. The movement has a verge escapement, pull repeat and a finely-engraved backplate.

Plate 52 Above left *A fine quality mahogany clock by John Leroux of Charing Cross, made in 1760. The broken dial is only 11" wide — a size which is rarely found.*
Centre *An important pair of George III clocks, made by Thomas Mudge and William Dutton, both eminent makers who were in partnership from 1755 – 1790. Thomas Mudge was apprenticed to George Graham who in turn was apprenticed to Tompion, and invented the lever escapement.*

Right *A typical late-eighteenth century pagoda-top mahogany longcase with 12" break-arch dial, by William Turner of London. The all-over silvered dial has a father time in the arch which rocks from side to side, being attached to the pendulum.*

into mere daubings of coloured paints and varnishes and cannot be compared with the earlier work which is usually of very high quality.

Unfortunately, owing to the fragile nature of lacquer, very few of the early cases have survived in good condition. The majority of lacquer cases were of pine construction and as this wood is very susceptible to attack from woodworm, only a small proportion of the clocks made in this style can have survived in their original state. It is also highly likely that a lot of the plain ebonized pine cases which are to be found with high quality movements were originally lacquered, and after the decoration had deteriorated, were then

Plate 53 Far left *A fine late-eighteenth century mahogany clock in the Mudge-and-Dutton style by another good maker, John Holmes, of the Strand, London. Circa 1785.*

Left *A provincial mahogany longcase clock by John Payne of Lenham, Kent. Circa 1785.*

stripped and coated black at some period in their life. Until recently, lacquer clocks were not as popular nor as expensive as the walnut and marquetry examples, mainly because of the shortage of good case restorers who work in this medium.

However, with the scarcity of the supplies of good quality examples in various veneers, they are now becoming sought after in their own right, and fine specimens are now fetching almost as much as the marquetry examples. They are especially popular in America and Germany.

Prior to 1700, dials, as has been previously stated, were usually no more than 11″ square. The cases of these clocks were normally never more than seven foot high and the mouldings to the hood base were convex in section. Sometime after the turn of the century it became fashionable to use a concave moulding and the cases themselves grew much taller, often with additional mouldings in the form of a caddy-top with finials, and examples are to be found up to 8′ 6″ in height. These taller clocks were obviously much more suited to the elegant interiors which had become fashionable in Queen Anne times and which lasted until the early Georgian period. At the same time as the concave moulding came into use, the pillars at the sides of the hood changed from the barley-sugar twist style to a plain doric type. With the increase in the dial size to 12″ came the next development of an archtop which often contained the maker's name on a silvered boss and in the later stages contained strike-silent mechanism or astronomical data such as tidal information or the stages of the moon.

In the early clocks the striking mechanism was of the outside count-wheel type and a detailed drawing is shown in Fig 8. At a later stage the count-wheel was moved between the plates and this can be seen in the illustration of a typical good-quality London movement of the 1695 period by John Finch, (Plate 35). Plate 36 shows the going train of this clock, and the ringed pillars holding the plates together, which are a particular feature of London clocks, can also be seen. The disadvantage of the count-wheel method of striking is that it is possible for the striking sequence to be upset, and in the event of this happening, it is necessary to let the clock strike by lifting the hammer shown in the diagrams until the locking device is in a comparable position on the count-wheel to the hour hand. In the latter part of the seventeenth century a more sophisticated method of striking was instituted, called rack-striking, following its invention by Edward Barlow and its application by Tompion, and the method was quickly adopted by the leading makers of the day. This method of striking made it impossible for the hour to be

Plate 54 Above *A good provincial longcase clock with a fine quality 8 day rack-striking movement, by D. Seddon of Frodsham, Cheshire, circa 1770. The 12″ dial has good engraving with a matted centre and subsidiary seconds and date aperture. The spandrels are the Four Seasons type which are commonly found in North Country clocks of the later eighteenth century.*

Plate 55 Right *Two country 8 day longcase clocks. The clock on the* **left** *has a 12″ dial and subsidiary seconds and calendar dials. Circa 1770. The clock on the* **right** *has mahogany crossbanding to the trunk door and a centre calendar hand. It dates from 1785.*

struck out of sequence with the hands, and thus did away with the necessity of letting the hours strike when altering the hands of the clock for any reason, and also made it possible for repeating work to be included in the mechanism. However, the count-wheel system continued to be used by many makers until very late in the eighteenth century, particularly in the country districts of England.

During the 1720's, mahogany began to be imported from the West Indies in ever-increasing quantities, and soon became a favourite wood of furniture makers and was extensively used for the cases of grandfather clocks, as they came to be known in the nineteenth century. Many of these cases are superb examples of cabinet work and made extensive use of the beautifully-figured veneers which could be obtained from the solid wood, particularly the Cuban variety.

Walnut furniture quickly went out of fashion after the arrival of mahogany, mainly because of the plentiful supplies of the latter and also because it was such a superb material with which to work. Most clockcases after 1730 are constructed of mahogany, although lacquered cases were still popular and remained so until the 1760's, even though the standard of the japanning showed a marked deterioration on the earlier examples. By this time the arch dial was the commonest form with strike/silent work in the arch. As has been previously mentioned, moon phases and tidal information were also often included. This information was obviously of great importance to a society whose trade was carried mostly by river and inland waterway and in an age when street lighting was non-existent.

During this period the clockmaking industry probably employed more people than any other, and almost every town and village in the country had one or more clockmakers. In some of the more remote villages clocks were often made by men in the spare time available from their main occupation of farming or shopkeeping. These country clocks were usually contained within oak cases and were often assembled from parts bought in from the specialist craftsmen in an industry that was becoming much more of a factory operation than in the past. It was the only way that the increasing demand could be met. Whilst many of the country makers produced fairly simple products, there is no doubt that many fine craftsmen existed in country areas. The Cockey family in Warminster, and Richard Comber from Lewes are just two of the Southern makers that spring to mind, and in the North the work of such men as Henry Hindly of York and Lister of Halifax could more than hold its own with the output of

Plate 56 Left *A very interesting longcase clock by an early Suffolk maker, Roger Moore of Ipswich. Whilst the case is typical of the 1770's, the 30 hour movement is of the early lantern style with turned posts framing the mechanism which has original minute work, subsidiary seconds and calendar work. The 10½″ brass and silver dial has fine engraving and original hands with cherub spandrels. Circa 1705. This clock was probably originally a hooded wall clock.*

the London makers.

As can be seen in Plates 26, 27, 28 and 29 great changes in the Longcase Dial took place particularly after 1700. Dials became very much more ornate after the adoption of the arched-dial with a consequent increase in the elaboration of the spandrel patterns. The early simple Cherub pattern gave way to the style utilising two cherubs holding a crown. Following this, a pattern of a mask's head surrounded by scroll-work was the commonest design on the Arch-dial used in conjunction with dolphins surrounding the boss in the arch.

This soon gave way to Rococo patterns which lasted until the inception of the all-silver dial in the 1770's, and the heralding of the arrival of mass-production methods with a consequent decrease in the standard of workmanship.

'Although the silver dial was still to be found in the late eighteenth century, the painted dial had now become very fashionable and the brass dial had almost disappeared. Case design in the provinces began to change quite dramatically, particularly in the North where cases became wider and squatter. To many people these cases, whilst being superbly made with fine inlaid work, are extremely ugly and do not have the attraction of the earlier elegant designs. What is strange is that cases in the South tended to be made in the earlier fashion except for Wales where cases followed the large Yorkshire and Lancashire examples. Early examples of the painted dial are recognisable by their simplicity, utilizing sprays of flowers painted directly onto the dial plate which was itself painted white with a faint greenish hue. These floral sprays took the place of the earlier brass spandrels. By 1800 coloured backgrounds to the floral design had become the fashion, together with the use of shell motifs or geometric patterns. Flower sprays were also painted in the arch where this dial shape was used, although paintings of birds are also often found. The dials were the work of the specialist artist and were attached to a false-plate which in turn was fixed to the main framework of the movement. The numerals on the earlier painted dials were usually painted in Roman style but during the 1800's Arabic figures began to be used instead. Dial painting became much more elaborate, often with local scenes, phases of the moon in the arch or moving ship automata. By 1800 the traditional style of longcase clock had ceased to be made in London and had been replaced by regulators which were mainly used for the purpose their name suggests, i.e. as a means of checking the timekeeping qualities of the output of the clockmaker who by this time was almost solely engaged in the manufacture of bracket clocks and watches.

Plate 57 Left *Typical English regulator of the Regency Period by Bracher of Sydenham.*

41

4. The development of the Bracket Clock

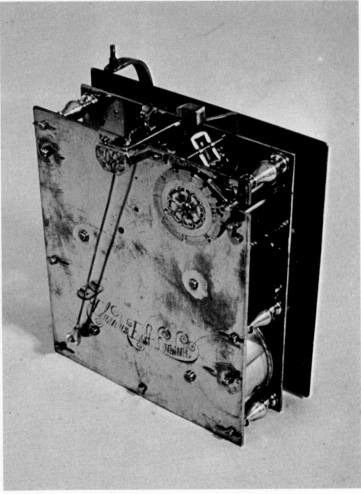

Plate 58 Opposite *A fine collection of bracket clocks and a good oak 30 hour longcase with 10" square dial and birdcage movement. By Baker of Malling, Kent, circa 1760.*
Display Cabinet
Top Row left *French red boulle clock, circa 1870.*
centre *English quarter chiming mahogany clock, by Ulrich, circa 1820.*
right *English rosewood mantel timepiece, circa 1830.*
Middle row left *German ting-tang quarter-chiming walnut bracket clock, circa 1870.*
centre *Fine ebonized bracket clock, by Morrison of Aberdeen, circa 1770.*
right *English Regency mahogany clock by Lister of Newcastle.*
Bottom Row left *Early-nineteenth century French four glass mantel clock*
centre *English mid-nineteenth century mahogany bracket clock*
right *Early nineteenth century French pillar clock with count wheel strike and gridiron pendulum.*

Plate 59 Top left *A very early ebony bracket clock by Edward East, with an 8 day striking movement with verge escapement. East was the finest of the early makers and was working in London from 1632 to 1693. He was Master of the Clockmaker's Company in 1645 and 1652.*

Plate 60 Bottom left *Detail of backplate and movement of an Edward East clock. Note the early vase-shaped pillars between the plates and the very simply-engraved backplate.*

Plate 61 Above *A very fine early pull/repeat bracket clock by the Yorkshire maker, John Rooksby, who is recorded as working in York in 1647. Note the fine engraving on the centre of the dial and the very unusual engraved spandrels.*

Whilst all these developments had been taking place in the field of the longcase clock, it must not be forgotten that bracket or table clocks were being produced at the same time. The early cases were architectural in style and were very similar to the hoods of the earliest longcase examples. Unlike the longcase clock, ebony-veneered or ebonized cases did not go out of fashion and continued to be used until the early years of the nineteenth century. Examples in wood veneers, mostly in walnut or kingwood, are to be found, and some marquetry and lacquered cases were also made. Mahogany was also used to great effect, and towards the end of the eighteenth century cases began to be inlaid with satinwood, and later in the Regency period were decorated with brass inlays. However, none of these finishes ousted the black case which remained the most popular fashion throughout the century.

The early style of case soon developed into the familiar basket-top design, and this fashion remained popular even after the inception of the bell-top case in the 1720's. The cases were usually embellished with pierced and gilded mounts, which in the finest examples were often solid silver or silver-gilt.

The main difference between the movements of the bracket and longcase clock is that the former uses the fusee movement in conjunction with the verge escapement and the bob pendulum. These clocks were usually placed on a table and were fitted with glass doors at the back of the clock so that the beautifully-engraved backplates could be seen to their best advantage, as can be seen from the illustrations in Plate 64 and 65. The early examples show a very strong Dutch influence with tulip designs around a centrally engraved maker's name. This developed into more intricate scrolled designs featuring faces of animals and birds and gave way to simpler floral patterns towards the end of the eighteenth century. With the degeneration in craftsmanship and the consequent lack of attention to detail which had been such a feature of the early makers, backplates ceased to be engraved after the 1800's except for the occasional edge-engraving which is to be found on clocks made by the better London makers.

The mechanism of the early bracket clocks often incorporated repeating work, enabling the previous hours and quarters to be struck on subsidiary bells by pulling a cord at the side of the case, thus enabling the time to be told in the dark and obviating the need to strike tinder boxes and light candles which were the only form of illumination. As a result of the supremacy of the English makers, a large demand grew up for their products abroad, particularly in China, Spain and Turkey. Some makers' business was almost exclusively with foreign countries and many examples of clocks with Turkish numerals exist. Other makers went to France to found a factory under a famous English maker, Henry Sully, but unfortunately this was not very successful and the traditional style of the English bracket and longcase clock was never very popular in France, where the more ornate style of clock, utilising ormulu and Boulle inlays was always more fashionable. Two fine examples of the French bracket clock of the 1700's are to be seen in Plates 71 and 72.

The bell-top and inverted bell-top style of case remained the most popular design for some 40 years until the advent of the break-arch style in the 1760's. An early clock of this type is shown in Plate 93 and later examples are shown in Plate 100.

The dials of bracket clocks exhibit similar

Plate 63 Above *A fine 8 day striking bracket clock by Christopher Gould of London, with calendar aperture and gilded mounts. The case of this clock is kingwood, veneered on oak. Circa 1695. Gould was a noted and prolific maker and worked from 1682 until 1718. Most of his work is characterised by his use of lavish decoration.*

Plate 62 Opposite *One of the finest clocks in the collection at the Victoria and Albert Museum: an early ebonized bracket clock in the architectural style by a noted early maker, Jeremie Gregorie, who was Free of the Clockmaker's Company in 1652 and Master in 1665. This magnificent clock with its gilt mounts and beautiful dial is thought to have been made for the Royal Exchange. Only three or four clocks by this maker are known to exist and a special point of interest is that the clock is signed on a name-plate as well as the more usual position at the foot of the dial-plate. Circa 1670.*

The Development of the Bracket Clock Back Plate

1680

1735

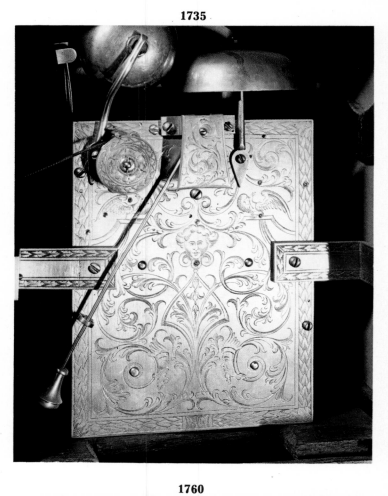

1780

1760

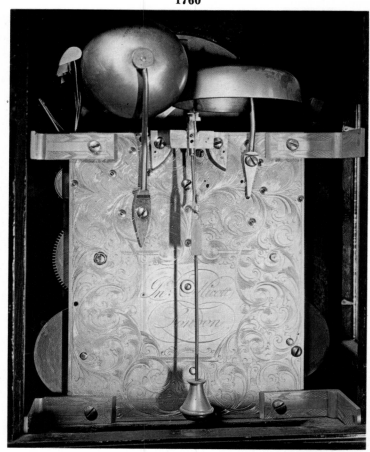

OPPOSITE 1690

Plate 67 Above *A late-seventeenth century ebonized bracket clock by the noted maker, Jonathan Lowndes of Pall Mall. This clock has a verge escapement and pull quarter repeat on a single bell. Both the spandrels and the engraving are of the highest quality. The backplate of this clock is shown on Page 47.*

Plate 66 Opposite *A late seveteenth century English bracket timepiece with pull quarter repeat on two bells with a verge escapement. The engraved backplate is signed Jacobus Goubert, London.*

Plate 68 Below *The smallest travelling clock so far recorded, made by Thomas Tompion. The case of this clock is only $6\frac{7}{16}$ high with a dial $3\frac{3}{8} \times 3\frac{3}{16}$. The case is ebony with silver mounts and silver spandrels to the dial. Although the clock is of miniature size, the movement is a standard Tompion type, with pull repeat and rise and fall regulation of the pendulum on the dial plate.*

Plate 69 Above *Another fine bracket clock in a seaweed marquetry case, made circa 1700 by John Martin of London.*

Plate 70 Below *A striking bracket clock in a kingwood veneered case by John Fromanteel, another member of this famous family of clockmakers. This clock is fitted with bolt and shutter maintaining power which is a device to keep the clock mechanism going by means of a spring even while it is being wound, in order to keep it accurate. The shutters covering the winding holes are moved aside by the lever at the base of the dial. This also actuates the spring mechanism.*

characteristics to the longcase variety, and the early clocks utilised cherub spandrels and hands of a similar pattern to those of the longcase clock. As the century progressed the changes in longcase dial design developed alongside the bracket clocks, although the standards of craftmanship of the latter seem to be so much higher. However, the change to enamel and silvered dials that took place in the 1770's heralded the beginning of the same decline in craftmanship and lack

Plates 71 and 72 Below and opposite page *Two fine examples of French bracket clocks of the Louis XIV period, circa 1700, in ormolu and boulle cases. French clocks were always far more ornate than their English counterparts and the more restrained style of the English bracket and longcase clock was never favoured in France where clocks were mainly desired for their furnishing rather than their time-keeping attributes.*

was no longer possible to produce work that had the same high finish at a competitive price. Another result of the increase in demand was that the manufacture of clocks was carried out by mass-production methods, almost exclusively by the end of the eighteenth century. This move towards mass-production had started very early on. In fact one of the reasons for the success of the great Thomas Tompion was that as early as the 1680's, he delegated certain tasks such as wheel cutting, plate of attention to detail as had happened with the longcase clock. The continually increasing demands of an ever more industrialised society meant that it making etc. to individual craftsman, thus speeding up the whole process. This method of working, together with his use of more advanced machinery, ie. the wheel-cutting engine, was the main reason for his large output of clocks and watches. As the century progressed, specialization increased rapidly to cater for the demands of what was a very large industry, employing 70,000 people out of a population of only 10 million by the end of the eighteenth century. The local clockmaker was able to purchase all the parts required from Birmingham, Liverpool and Clerkenwell in London, which were now the main centres of production; this accounts for the similarity of so many movements bearing the names of different clockmakers of this period.

The advance of industrialization meant that it was no longer possible to pay such close attention to detail and this is most apparent when one looks at spandrels in particular. The early cherub styles were individually cast, then chased by hand and finally gilded and burnished. The later examples were very rarely polished and the amount of hand finishing was minimal.

Although the bracket clock continued to be popular for many years, the production of longcase clocks had declined in London, although they continued to be made in the provinces and the whole industry now suffered a blow from which it never really recovered.

In 1797 to help raise revenue towards the cost of the Napoleonic Wars, William Pitt imposed an annual tax on clocks and watches. The tax varied from 10 shillings (50 pence) on a gold watch to 2s 6d (12½ pence) for a 30 hour longcase clock. Owing to its unpopularity this Act was repealed only nine months later, but alas, the damage had been done: thousands of clockmakers were thrown out of work and the decline in the English clockmaking industry had begun in earnest.

A strange side-effect of this Act is that today the 'Tavern' clock, examples of which can be seen on Page

Plates 73 and 74 Overleaf *Two fine early Georgian red lacquer bracket clocks. The clock on the **left** has strike/silent mechanism and is housed in an arched bell-top case which superseded the basket style seen on earlier clocks. This example is circa 1725. The clock on the **right** is a fine musical clock in an inverted bell-top case, with strike/silent work and tune selection on the two subsidiary dials in the arch. Made by Charles Bosley circa 1750.*

Plate 75 Top left *Good quality arch dial clock in bell-top ebonized case, circa 1735, by the famous maker John Ellicott. The movement has a verge escapement and pull quarter repeat on six bells, and very fine spandrels. Ellicott, who invented a compensating pendulum and developed the cyclinder escapement for watches, was also a fellow of the Royal Society, and clockmaker to George II and George III.*

Plate 76 Bottom left *Another clock by this maker, circa 1760, with a three train quarter striking movement on eight bells.*

66, are now popularly called 'Act of Parliament' clocks. It was thought that because of this Act private individuals disposed of their clocks, and as a result large wall clocks were mounted in taverns and other public buildings to take their place. This is not the case as weight-driven clocks of this type had been in existence since the 1740's and were the direct descendants of the earlier Turret clocks.

Plate 77 Above *A fine George II period ebonized bracket clock with pull quarter repeat on six bells, by William Kipling of London.*

Plate 78 Opposite *A very fine yellow lacquer three train clock, made for the Turkish market. Note the Turkish numerals and crescent motif on the hands. A flourishing export trade grew up between England and other countries in the early-eighteenth century, notably Turkey, Spain, China and Scandinavia. This example is by William Dunnant, who was working in London before 1760.*

Plate 79 Opposite page *A superb 8 day three train musical bracket clock by Nathaniel Barnes of London, circa 1780. The case has fine gilt mounts and is veneered with tortoiseshell.*

Plate 80 Top left *A later eighteenth century ebonised bracket clock with a quarter striking musical movement playing a selection of four tunes every hour. By George Clarke, London, circa 1770.*

Plate 81 Bottom left *An ebonized verge bracket clock by Morrison of Aberdeen, with adjustment for pendulum rise and fall (for time-keeping), top left of dial, and strike/silent regulation at top right. Circa 1770.*

Plate 83 Above *An 8 day striking bracket clock in a mahogany case with gilt mounts, by Yeldrae Notron of London, circa 1790. The signature is an anagram for Eardley Norton, a famous late-eighteenth century maker.*

Plate 84 Left *An ebonized bracket clock with an enclosed silver dial by Joseph Herring, circa 1770. This style of case is supposed to have been first used by the famous maker John Ellicott.*

Plate 85 Left centre *A late eighteenth century bracket clock in a mahogany case by Thomas Percival of London. This clock has a silvered dial with spandrels and strike/silent and seconds dials in the arch. Circa 1790.*

Plate 87 Below *Another version of this style of case. An ebonized clock with chapter ring and spandrels and matting on the centre of the dial. By Percival Mann, London. Circa 1770.*

Plate 86 Left *A very early example of the break-arch style of bracket clock with a circular dial enclosed by the case door. By William Bull of Stratford. Circa 1770.*

Plates 88 and 89 Right *Two views of a fine ebonized clock with a quarter-repeating movement, by William Scafe of London. Note the unusual position of the signature on the dialplate and the very fine engraving on the backplate and pendulum. Circa 1750.*

Plates 90 and 91 Opposite bottom right *A very fine late eighteenth century mahogany bracket clock by Florimond Goddard, circa 1780, with very fine engraving on the backplate and the pendulum.*

Plate 93 Above *A superb musical and grand-sonnerie striking bracket clock by Eardley Norton, London, circa 1790. The gilt and copper case has enamelled dials and a painted rural scene in the arch.*

Plate 92 Left *A late-eighteenth century walnut clock with its original bracket from the famous family of clockmakers, Ellicott. Circa 1770.*

Plate 94 Below *Three examples of the late-eighteenth century style of bracket clock. Circa 1790.*
Left *Mahogany example by John Baker, London, with half dead-beat escapements and subsidiary strike/silent work and a painted enamel dial.*
Right *Mahogany clock by John Levens, London, with a brass and silvered dial.*
Centre *Ebonised bracket clock by John Gale of London, with porcelain enamelled dial.*

5. Technical advances in the eighteenth century

Whilst all these changes in case styles and designs were taking place, there were great technical advances also. In 1715 George Graham, one of the most famous names in the history of the craft and the successor to Tompion, invented the dead-beat escapement. This form of the anchor escapement did away with the recoil of the earlier design and made it possible to produce an even more accurate timepiece which became known as a regulator. He also developed the mercury pendulum to counteract the expansion which took place in a metal pendulum during temperature changes, which resulted in variations in accuracy, (fig. 11). The level of the mercury rose or fell with the rise and fall in temperature countering the changes in the length of the pendulum rod.

Another famous maker, John Harrison, also developed a more accurate version which has come to be known as the gridiron or compensated pendulum. This uses alternate brass and steel rods and utilises the different rates of expansion of the two metals to produce a constant pendulum length (fig. 11) Harrison was also responsible for the development of the marine chronometer which solved the problem of finding longitude. This was one of the tasks assigned to the Greenwich observatory on its foundation in 1675, but it

Plate 95 Above *A pair of regency bracket clocks in brass inlaid ebonized cases with chamfer tops. The better quality example is on the* **right** *with a silvered dial and signed Purvis on the dial and backplate. Circa 1820. The clock on the left is a strike/silent example with a painted dial, by Dent of London, and has an engraved border to the backplate.*

Plate 96 Below *A matching pair of mahogany lancet top bracket clocks by Barwise of London, with Egyptian mounts, circa 1800. The influence of classical and Egyptian designs in household decoration and furniture and clock case design spread rapidly during the Regency period, following the publication in 1807 of a book of designs by Thomas Hope, a noted scholar and architect. The vogue for Egyptian decoration was at its height during the first ten years of the nineteenth century.*

Figure 10 *The dead-beat escapement.*

Plate 97 Above *A very fine 'balloon' cased ebonized clock with brass mounts by a noted maker, J. Leroux of London, with a silvered dial. Circa 1770.*

Plate 98 Below *A late eighteenth century ebonized bracket clock by James McCabe, with a painted dial and good hands. Circa 1790. The picture on the **right** shows the backplate of this clock with the simple edge-engraving which was now common practice instead of the earlier, more florid style of engraving. James McCabe was a very fine maker who died in 1811, but whose business was carried on by his sons until 1883.*

was not until Harrison's invention in 1759 of a chronometer which gave an error of only five seconds, (1½ miles) on a voyage to Jamaica, that the problem was finally solved. The son of a carpenter had tried to resolve the problem for some years and had made three earlier timekeepers which had been turned down by the Admirality. The 'Harrison's No. 4', as it has come to be known, which was used on the voyage, was basically a large watch, incorporating sophisticated devices for dealing with changes in temperature, and a remontoire, a device which rewound the spring every 7½ seconds, keeping its pull constant. With this design he won a prize of £20,000 which had first been offered by the government in 1714, and helped to ensure the supremacy of the British Navy during the rest of the eighteenth century. Further developments in marine chronometer design were made by another famous maker, Thomas Mudge, a former apprentice of the great George Graham. However, both Mudge and Harrison's instruments were far too complicated for general use, and the English lead in the production of chronometers for general use at sea was mainly due to the further work carried out by Thomas Earnshaw and John Arnold. Two fine examples of 19th century marine chronometers are shown on pages 64 and 65.

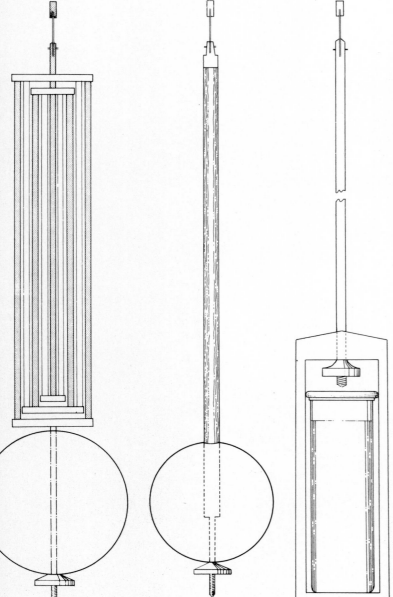

Plate 100 Left *A good strike/repeat bracket clock in another version of the 'balloon' shaped case. This case is veneered with partridge wood and has satinwood and box-wood inlays. By Brown of Charing Cross, circa 1800.*

Plate 101 Below *A superb regency bracket clock with a stepped-top ebonized pearwood veneered case with brass inlay. The strike/repeat movement is by Barrand of Cornhill, London, and has a signed and edge-engraved backplate. Circa 1810.*

Plate 102 Overleaf left *A small size two day chronometer by a good firm of Liverpool clockmakers, Litherland Davies & Co. circa 1825.*

Plate 103 Overleaf right *A fine quality two day chronometer by Parkinson and Frodsham circa 1830, in a mahogany case.*

Figure 11 Left *Harrison's grid-iron pendulum. The steel rods are longer than the brass to utilise the greater expansion qualities of brass. Thus the length of the pendulum remains constant.* **Centre** *Wood-rod pendulum.*
Right *Graham's mercury compensated pendulum.*

Eighteenth & Nineteenth Century Wall Clocks

Plate 104 Above *A lantern clock with a verge escapement, made for the Turkish market, circa 1780 by Markwick Markham of London. Note the Turkish crescent moon incorporated in the spandrels and the Turkish numerals. This firm of clockmakers had a thriving export market with Turkey and made many fine bracket clocks.*

Plate 105 Below *Black lacquer tavern clock with an eight day movement by Robert Allam of London, circa 1770. The smaller wall-clock is nineteenth century English 'drop-dial' in a carved walnut case with a striking fusee movement.*

Plate 106 Above *A very fine early 'Act of Parliament' lacquer clock by Pratt of West Hampton, circa 1760. This clock has a very good plated movement with ringed pillars. Also note the unusual base to the trunk. Although these clocks are popularly called 'Act of Parliament' clocks, after William Pitt's introduction of a tax on clocks and watches in 1797, they had been in existence for some years before this and were known as Tavern clocks. The majority of the early examples had lacquer decoration similar to the two clocks featured on this page.*

Plate 107 Above *A very rare wall-mounted striking musical clock of the early eighteenth century, by Joseph Phillips of Bristol. This clock has a calendar aperture and superb hands and cherub spandrels with central matting on the dial.*

Plate 108 Above *A rear view of this clock showing the massive four post lantern construction and large double fusee barrels chiming on eight bells.*

Plate 109 Below *A fine quality striking wall clock by a noted maker, Alexander Cumming, with a silvered dial and calendar work, in a mahogany case. Circa 1770.*

Plate 110 Above right *Two wall clocks with fusee movement, the smaller one with an 8″ dial, by Walker of South Molton Street circa 1900 and the earlier example by Lilly of Poole, circa 1840. Both are in mahogany cases.*

Above left *A fine wall-mounted regulator with half-seconds movement, by David, circa 1800.*

6. French clocks of the later eighteenth century

The clockmaking industry in France had continued to flourish until the seventeenth century under the direction of the Paris Guilds which controlled standards and conditions of work in a similar fashion to the clockmakers' company in England. Many fine early clocks were produced both in Paris and the provincial centres such as Lyons and Marseille; some fine examples are shown in Chapter 1 of this volume. However, during the seventeenth century the fashion for wearing watches on the person swept the country and there was such a dramatic decline in clock production that the industry in France had virtually ceased to exist by 1653 and the accession of Louis XIV to the Throne. Following the introduction of the pendulum, clocks in France followed the Dutch designs in their use of ebony veneers and because of their sombre-looking cases were known as 'Pendules Religeuse'. This style of clock was completely out of keeping with the elaborate classical style of decoration which came into favour in France under the rule of 'The Sun King', Louis XIV. As a result, the ornate style of clock, inlaid with tortoiseshell and boulle decoration, soon found favour, and as a style lasted until the end of the century; in fact the design was re-introduced in the late 19th century and remains popular to the present day.

Plate 111 Top Left *An English clock made of white marble with gilt mounts in this French style, by Vulliamy of London, with a numbered and signed movement, No. 246, circa 1785. Members of this family of great clockmakers made many fine clocks throughout the middle and late eighteenth century and Benjamin Vulliamy was clockmaker to George III.*

Plate 112 Left *A highly decorative boulle clock with gilt mounts and enamelled figures on the dial, by Langlois of Paris. Late eighteenth century.*

Plate 113 Right *Another fine marble and ormolu-mounted clock of this period.*

Plate 114 Overleaf left *A very fine ormolu clock with an enamelled painted dial, by Voisin à Paris. Circa 1775.*

Plate 115 Overleaf right *A white marble and ormolu clock of the Louis XVI period, by De Belle, with calendar work. Circa 1780.*

Plate 116 Top left *A French ormolu mantel clock by Barraud à Paris, of the Louis XVI period, circa 1785.*

Plate 117 Bottom left *Another fine Louis XVI ormolu clock by Le Masurier à Paris. Circa 1780*

Plate 118 Below *An early nineteenth century Austrian ormolu mounted clock with a French movement, circa 1810. Note the centre calendar hand showing the days of the month.*

Plate 119 Opposite page *A very fine marble and gilt clock with an enamelled painted dial with unusual hands. This clock was made in Paris by Lejeune, circa 1790.*

The longcase clock was never popular in France where the large, ornate spring-driven clock on a matching base was much more fashionable and more in keeping with the lavishly decorated interiors. Towards the end of the eighteenth Century, rococo-styled waisted bracket clocks became very popular until the advent of the simpler Marble clocks with enamel dials, showing a classical influence. After the Revolution of 1789 the craft guilds were disbanded, but business was stimulated by the introduction of industrial exhibitions in Paris, the first of which took place in 1797. The classical influence was further strengthened by the ideas brought back from the Middle East following the crowning of Napoleon as Emperor in 1804 and the introduction of Empire style furniture with its mixture and use of Egyptian and classical forms and motifs.

7. The nineteenth century

During the early years of the industry, the very strict standards insisted upon by the Clockmakers' Company had helped the English makers to become the best in the world. However, as the eighteenth century progressed the influence of the Company decreased, and had very little effect on the industry outside of London by the 1800's, except that the traditional attitude to high standards of workmanship which it had fostered and encouraged for so many years, led to a resistance to extreme mass-production methods.

A direct result of this was the inability of the English trade to compete with the cheaper spring-driven clocks which began to flood into the country from **France**, Germany and America during the nineteenth century and in particular after the Great Exhibition of 1851.

By 1830 the beginning of the age of the railway had greatly hastened the spread of industry throughout the country and Britain was soon to become the World's first fully industrialised society, with a working population whose lives were governed by the clock, and the necessity for good timekeeping accelerated the huge demand for clocks and watches. The inability of the English clockmakers to fulfill this demand, both on the grounds of cost and adequate supplies, coincided with the free trade policies of the Liberals under Gladstone and the removal of import duties. All these factors were disastrous to the British clockmaking industry. In 1854, to take just one year's figures, the staggering number of 228,000 clocks were imported into the country, the vast majority being French mantel clocks in marble and ornamental cases.

By 1851 there was added competition from the rapidly-growing American industry where mass-production methods enabled makers such as Chauncey Jerome, Seth Thomas and the Ansonia Clock Company to produce spring-driven shelf clocks for as little as two dollars! In their effort to capture the world market they copied many European designs, including the ubiquitous French marble clock. In this instance they used enamelled iron or painted wood to imitate the marble cases, and their cheap copies of Dutch clocks of the time resulted in the virtual demise of Holland's clockmaking industry.

At the Great Exhibition of 1851 many of the medals awarded were given to firms who introduced methods to cut the costs of production, but in spite of this some clocks were still being produced using the old skills and to the old standards. There was also a revival of many of the earlier styles, particularly the French bracket clock with boulle decoration and the large ebonized clock with ormolu mounts by English firms such as E.J. Dent

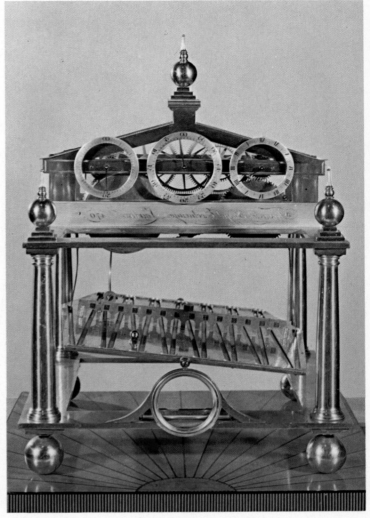

Plate 121 Above *The 'Congreve' rolling ball timepiece, made by French of the Royal Exchange, circa 1810, from a design patented by Sir William Congreve, F.R.S. in 1808. The steel ball takes 30 seconds to roll from one end of the table to the other. At each end a catch is released, enabling the spring-driven movement to tip the table the other way. The mainspring has to be wound every 21 days. It has been calculated that the ball travels 2,500 miles each year. This clock is part of the collection at the British Museum.*

Plate 120 Opposite Page *A close-up of a very fine gilt-brass and enamelled dial of a French eighteenth century clock in a tortoiseshell and boulle inlaid case.*

(the makers of 'Big Ben'). However, as with so many of the Victorian revivals, their desire for so-called 'improvement' often led them to produce over-complicated designs with an abundance of vulgar decorative detail far removed from the cases they endeavoured to copy.

During this period other forms of clock became fashionable, notably skeleton and carriage clocks. The first of these had their mechanisms open to view under a glass dome and some good examples are pictured on pages 82 and 83. Many of these clocks were made to represent English Cathedrals, St Paul's in London, and

Lichfield with its three spires, were often copied.

The ever-popular carriage clock had been made in France since the 1830's where it was known as the 'Pendule de Voyage'. Some fine examples were made from this time also, by the better-known English makers such as James McCabe, Dent and Charles Frodsham. These employed the fusee method of escapement and were much larger than the French type which used a platform escapement. However the vast majority of these clocks were of French origin, with a case of four pillars, glass panels, a hinged carrying handle and a leather-covered travelling box. Many of the cases were superbly decorated and engraved and varied from plain timepieces to grand-sonnerie examples which strike the hours and quarters; repeating-work and alarm mechanism are also a common feature. These carriage clocks are now amongst the most sought after by today's purchasers, probably because of their small size and their main asset of blending with any style of interior decoration.

Whilst the ordinary marble mantel clock has been object of derision for many years, and was totally ignored by all antique dealers (except for those dealing in 'junk'), they are now steadily increasing in price, and a good example in a pretty case will now fetch between £40 and £85. All of these clocks had very good French movements and with the ever-increasing scarcity of the early clocks, not to mention the sky-high prices, they can only continue to increase in value.

During the Victorian era, the early productions of the great craftsmen of the eighteenth century were much despised, and in many instances fine longcase and bracket clocks were relegated to the attic. It is only in recent years that they have come to be appreciated as supreme examples of English skills and works of art in their own right. Even famous makers of the nineteenth century, such as Vulliamy, who made very fine clocks, had little regard for the work of early clockmakers and there are many instances of clocks by makers such as Tompion having their movements replaced — acts which are now regarded as vandalism — in the same way that so many churches were 'improved' by the Victorian architect, much to their detriment.

Fortunately, in spite of the declining standards of workmanship, there are still people specialising in restoring these old masterpieces to something approaching their original condition. The Antiquarian Horological Society* has done much to foster this

*The Antiquarian Horological Society, New House, High Street, Ticehurst, Wadhurst, Sussex

Plate 122 Opposite *A very fine Victorian bracket clock by R. & W. Sorley of Glasgow, in the form of a temple. The case is made of Loromandel wood with fine gilt mounts and fretwork. Circa 1860.*

Plate 123 Top right *A nineteenth century French clock with a gilt and boulle decorated case.*

Plate 124 Right *A French ormolu clock with an enamelled and painted dial of the Louis Philippe period, circa 1830.*

77

interest and membership is recommended to anybody who becomes interested in clocks and clockmaking, if only because of the information contained in its quarterly journal. In addition, they have also encouraged and fostered the reprinting of many publications which have long been out of print.

In common with the rest of the antique world, clocks have captured the attention of the fakers, and it is good sense for any prospective purchaser to buy from a specialist clock dealer rather than from a general antique dealer. Not only will the specialist have a more detailed knowledge of the subject, but also a much larger stock which will have been restored by competent craftsmen whose work will usually be guaranteed by any reputable dealer.

Unfortunately, in the world of clocks, as in the antique business generally, good clocks are becoming harder and harder to find. Thousands of fine examples have been shipped abroad, and not just the work of the leading makers, the prices of which are now beyond the

Plate 125 Top left *A very unusual English timepiece with a fusee movement, in a black slate case modelled on an Egyptian temple showing the Thomas Hope classical influence in case design persisting until the 1840's. The very fine engine-turned dial is signed by Arnold but the backplate has Charles Frodsham's signature.*

Plate 128 Above *Two typical regulators of the middle and late nineteenth century. The clock on the* **left** *has a grand-sonnerie movement and is housed in a fine walnut case.*

Plates 126 and 127 Centre left and left *Two examples of nineteenth century English dial clocks, both with fusee movements. The octagonal clock has a rosewood case with brass inlay.*

Plate 129 Opposite *A large Victorian chiming bracket clock in an ebonized case with gilt mounts. This clock has strike/silent work and a choice of either Cambridge or Westminster chimes. Circa 1880.*

reach of all but the most affluent. Good oak country clocks with 30 hour and 8-day brass-dialed movements are highly sought after by foreign dealers, as are the later clocks with painted dials, particularly those with automata in the dial arch. These clocks are rapidly increasing in price and are getting scarcer all the time as we gradually become aware that our heritage is disappearing to Holland, Belgium, Germany and America, with no possibility of their return to this country whilst exchange rates remain as they are at present.

Anybody who is thinking of purchasing a clock, even if only as a piece of furniture or decoration, is strongly recommended to do so in the very near future whilst they are still to be found. As in the case of many other antique articles, clocks have also attracted the attention

Plate 130 Top left *A marble 'mystery' clock, circa 1870, with a gilded figure holding the pendulum and a good engine-turned dial.*

Plate 131 Left *A procelain version of a clock more usually seen in a bronze or ormolu finish.*

Plate 132 Above *Another late nineteenth century French ormolu clock in an elaborate case.*

Plate 133 Opposite page *A French boulle clock of the late nineteenth century, made in the style of a hundred years earlier.*

English Skeleton Clocks

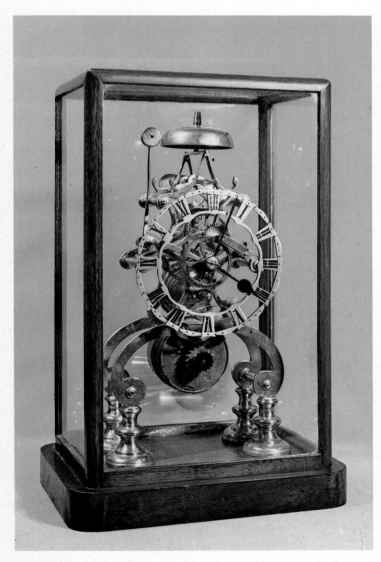

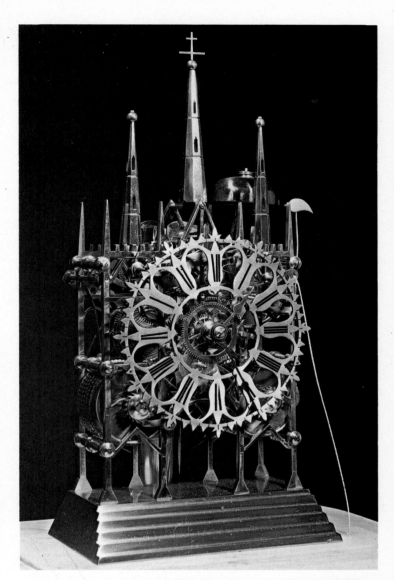

Plate 136 Top right *An English skeleton clock in the shape of Lichfield Cathedral, striking the hours on a gong and a passing quarter-strike on a bell, with a mercurial compensated pendulum. Circa 1870.*

Plate 135 Above *A good-quality English skeleton clock timepiece movement with passing strike. Circa 1865.*

Plate 137 Right *Another English nineteenth century skeleton clock, probably made by Smiths, circa 1860.*

Plate 134 Opposite *A very fine English gilt skeleton clock on a marble base, modelled on St. Pauls Cathedral. Circa 1860.*

Plates 138 and 139 *Two very rare early French carriage clocks by Paul Garnier. The example* **above** *was made circa 1835 and has a two-piece escapement with lift-up front glass for winding.*

Below *This is a strike/repeat clock with a musical alarm on two airs, also with a two plane escapement. Circa 1840.*

Plate 140 Opposite page *A superb large size English carriage clock with a quarter striking fusee movement. This clock was probably made by Charles Frodsham for Klaftenberger of Regent Street, circa 1850.*

of the speculator who is not necessarily interested in them for himself but merely as another commodity to be dealt in for profit. This has again helped to push up the prices of all types of clocks and although there was a slump in the more highly-priced items three years ago, this did not affect those made by the lesser makers which are steadily increasing in value as more and more people realise that perhaps it is better to have an object of beauty and great usefulness which they can enjoy possessing, rather than money which is constantly devaluing in a sterile bank account.

During the past few years, more and more fine clocks have found their way into museums, and in this country we are particularly fortunate in having a number of superb collections. Anybody who has the smallest interest in the subject should make a point of visiting the Victoria and Albert Museum where a number of fine clocks can be seen in their rightful settings in the rooms devoted to English furniture. The finest collection of all is that of the British Museum who managed to acquire the famed Ilbert Collection a few years ago, numbering more than 350 examples and which can be seen in the Clock and Watch department. Other fine collections are at the Science Museum, and the collection belonging to the Clockmakers' Company is now housed in The Guildhall Museum, in the City of London.

Whilst the best examples are nearly all in the capital, most of the provincial museums hold a number of good clocks among their other exhibits, particularly the City of Liverpool Museum, the Fitzwilliam Museum in Cambridge and the Ashmolean Museum in Oxford. Many fine collections are to be found throughout Europe and the United States, and a detailed list of locations is given at the end of this volume together with an extensive bibliography.

Plate 141 Opposite page top row *Three very fine large French carriage clocks.*
Far left *An example by Drocourt, 9½" high with a grand-sonnerie and alarm movement, circa 1860.* **Centre** *A grand-sonnerie clock by de Jardin in a fully-engraved case. This clock strikes on two bells. Circa 1850.*
Right *another by Drocourt in a 10" high gorge case with strike/repeat movement. The dial is signed by Benson who retailed the clock.*

Middle row
Right *An early carriage clock by Japy Freres in a one piece case with a solid shuttered back door. The movement has a lever escapement and a finely-engraved platform, with strike/repeat and alarm work and centre seconds hands. Circa 1860.*

Centre *A gorge cased repeating carriage clock with subsidiary dials for calendar and alarm with a finely-engraved surround on the dial, by Drocourt of Paris, 1870.*

Left *A similar clock to the Japy Frere already described. This clock is also by Japy, but has an engraved case. Circa 1860.*

Bottom row left *Three views of a fine grand sorrerie clock by Henri Jacot, circa 1870, with enamelled painted panels on the case.*

Plate 144 Above *A good French carriage clock of the mid-nineteenth century by the well-known Paris maker, Japy Freres. The case has very fine engraving and a strike/repeat movement with alarm work. Also note the centre seconds hand which was a common feature on clocks made for the Chinese market.*

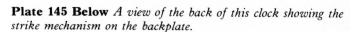

Plate 145 Below *A view of the back of this clock showing the strike mechanism on the backplate.*

Plate 143 Left *Another strike/repeat carriage clock in an engraved oval case with an engine-turned dial. Circa 1870.*

87

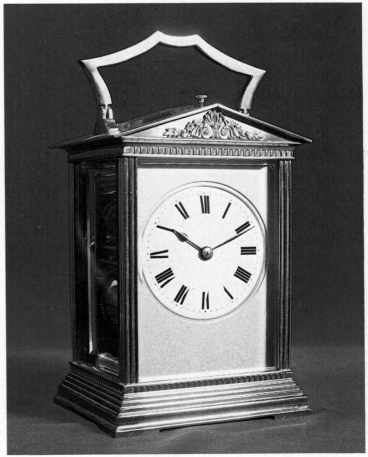

Plate 147 Above *Nineteenth century mantel regulator with subsidiary dials for day, date, month, sunrise, sunset, equation of time and moon phases. Circa 1850*

Plate 148 Top right *A silver petit sonnerie carriage clock with an enamel dial and gilt hands. Circa 1870.*

Plate 149 Right *A large gilt French clock with a strike/repeat movement in an unusual architectural style case. From the same period.*

Plate 146 Opposite page *A very unusual French carriage clock with an eight-day strike/repeat movement. The bamboo style gilt case has its original enamel panels with hand-painted pictures of nesting birds and dates from 1870.*

Plate 152 Top left *Mid-nineteenth century month duration table regulator by Thomas Cole, with manually operated perpetual calender, case veneered in coromandel wood and ebony.*

Plate 153 Above *A very fine French carriage clock by the well-known maker, Drocourt of Paris, in an engraved case with a grand-sonnerie movement. Circa 1870.*

Plate 152 Above *Two examples of nineteenth century carriage clocks in the popular gorge case style. The clock on the **right** has a strike/repeat movement and is by Brocot of Paris, circa 1870.*

Plate 150 Opposite page *A magnificent large English carriage clock by Deni of London, chiming on eight bells, with full perpetual calendar work and a chronometer escapement. Circa 1897. The firm of Dent made the clock for the Houses of Parliament, popularly known as 'Big Ben'.*

List of Clockmakers featured in the Book

ALLAM, ROBERT, London. Apprenticed 1730 CC 1742-1765 Plate 105

BAKER, HENRY, Malling, Kent. Circa 1705-1780 Plate 58

BAKER, JOHN, London (Covent Garden). Apprenticed 1768 CC 1781-1799 Plate 94

BANGER, EDWARD, London. Apprenticed to Thomas Tompion in 1687. Married Tompion's niece Margaret Kent, & subsequently taken into partnership. Many clocks exist signed Tompion & Banger. CC 1695-1713 Plate 39

BARNES, NATHANIEL, London. Circa 1780 Plate 79

BARRAUD, PAUL PHILIP, London (Cornhill). Master CC 1810-1811. Died 1820 Plate 101

BARWISE, JOHN, London. Died 1842 CC 1790 Plate 96

BOSLEY, CHARLES, London. Apprenticed 1725 CC 1749 Plate 74

BOWYER, WILLIAM, London. Working between 1626-1647. One of the Founder-members of the Clock-makers' Company Plate 21

BROWN, JOHN, London (Charing Cross). 1785-1811 Plate 100

BULL, WILLIAM, London (Stratford). 1770-1804 Plate 86

BURGESS, ELIAS, London. Apprenticed 1673 CC 1681-1702 Plate 48

CARTWRIGHT, THOMAS, London. Apprenticed 1693 Died 1743. Watchmaker to Queen Anne and George I Plate 41

CLARKE, GEORGE, London. CC 1725-1787 Plate 80

CUMMING, ALEXANDER, Edinburgh & London. Born 1732, died 1814. A famous clockmaker Plate 109

DE BELLE, JEAN F., Paris. 1780 — early 19th century Plate 115

DENT, EDWARD J., London. Born 1790 d. 1853 A famous maker Plates 95 & 150

DUNNANT, WILLIAM, London. Recorded as working before 1760 Plate 78

DUTTON, WILLIAM, London. Apprenticed in 1738. Partner of Thomas Mudge & took over the business in 1771. A famous maker CC 1746 Plate 52

EAST, EDWARD, London. Circa 1610 Master of Clockmakers' Co. 1645 & 1652. D. 1693. One of the most famous of the early makers CC 1632 Plates 59 & 60

ELLIOTT, THOMAS, Greenwich. Recorded as working before 1715 Plate 45

EBSWORTH, JOHN, London. Apprenticed 1657 Master of Company 1697-1703 A noted maker CC 1665 Plate 28

ELLICOTT, JOHN, London (Swithin's Alley Royal Exchange). Born 1706 D. 1772 Fellow of the Royal Society & one of the foremost clockmakers Plates 50, 75, 76 & 92

FINCH, JOHN, London. Apprenticed in 1668. Master 1706 D. 1713 CC 1675 Plates 27, 35, 36

FIRSTENFELDER B., Friedburg. Late 17th Century Plate 11

FROMANTEEL, A., London. Member of the Blacksmith's Co. in 1630 introduced the pendulum to England. A very famous maker CC 1632 Plates 22, 23 & 24

FROMANTEEL, J., London. Apprenticed 1651 Worked with Salomon Coster from Sept. 1657 to May 1658 on his return to England his father Ahasuerus advertised the first pendulum clock. CC 1663-1681 Plate 70

FRENCH, S.J., London (Royal Exchange). CC 1810-1840 Plate 121

FRY, Kilmersdon. Circa 1740 Plate 48

FRODSHAM, CHARLES, London (Finsbury Pavement & Strand). Master CC 1855 A very good maker. Succeeded John Roger Arnold in 1843, CC 1854 Plate 125 & 140

GALE, JOHN, London. 1790-1840 Plate 94

GODDARD, FLORIMOND, London. 1780-1797 Plate 90 & 91

GODFREY, HENRY, London. CC 1685-1707 Plate 33

GOUBERT, JACOBUS, London. CC 1690-1701 Plate 66

GOULD, CHRISTOPHER, London. Died 1718 A noted maker CC 1682 Plates 30-63

GARNIER, PAUL, Paris. 19th Century. A famous clockmaker particularly of carriage clocks Plates 138-139

GREGORIE, JEREMIE, London (Royal Exchange Cornhill). Master CC 1665 Died 1685 A noted early maker CC 1652 Plate 62

GRETTON, CHARLES, London The Ship, Fleet Street. Apprenticed 1662 Master 1701 A Noted maker CC 1672 Plate 1

HARE, ALEXANDER, London. Apprenticed 1776 CC 1781-1824 Plate 50

HARRIS, STEPHEN, Tonbridge. Recorded as working circa 1690-1730 Plate 41

HARPER, HENRY, London (Cornhill). Apprenticed 1657 Died 1708 CC 1664 Plate 34

HASIUS, JACOB, Amsterdam. Working from 1682 until 1725 Plate 32

HERRING, JOSEPH, London. CC 1767-1804 Plate 84

HOLMES, JOHN, London (The Strand). 1762-1815 A famous maker Plate 53

JACKEMAN, JOSEPH, London Bridge. 1682-1716 Plate 40

JOHNSON, BENJAMIN, London. Recorded as working 1693-1720 Plate 31

JONES, HENRY, London (Temple). Apprenticed 1645 Master CC 1691 Died 1695 A famous maker CC 1663 Plates 27 & 64

KIPLING, WILLIAM, London. Working from 1705-1737 A fine maker Plate 77

KNIBB, JOSEPH, Oxford & London. Working in Oxford 1650. Probably working in London from 1677 and Hanslip from 1700. Died 1711. One of the greatest clockmakers. CC 1670 Plate 44

LEROUX, JOHN, London (Charing Cross). Working from 1744 A noted maker CC 1781-1808 Plates 52 & 97

List of Clockmakers featured in the Book

LEVENS, JOHN, London (Shoemakers Row). Apprenticed 1752 CC 1761-1807 Plate 94
LILLY W.C., Poole. 1848-1855 Plate 110
LISTER, WILLIAM, Newcastle-on-Tyne. 1815-1820 Plate 58
LITHERLAND, DAVIES & CO., Liverpool. 1818-1837 Plate 102
LOUBET, FELIX, Paris. 2nd Half 16th Century Plate 8
LOWNDES, J. London (Pall Mall). A famous maker CC 1680-1710 Plates 30, 67
MARKHAM, MARKWICK, London. Circa 1725 — Circa 1805 Partnership of two good clockmakers, Robert Markham & James Markwick. Master CC 1720. D.1730 CC 1692 Plate 104
MARKWICK, JAMES, London. Master CC 1720 Died 1730. An eminent maker. CC 1692 Plate 47
MARTIN, JOHN, London. Apprenticed 1672 CC 1679-1701 Plate 69
MITCHELL & MOTT, New York. Circa 1790-1809 Plate 51
MORRISON, GEORGE, Aberdeen. Circa 1792 Plates 58 & 81
MOORE, ROGER, Ipswich. Circa 1690-1720 Father of Thomas Moore. A noted Suffolk maker Plate 56
MUDGE, THOMAS, London. Born 1715. Apprenticed to George Graham. Died 1794. A very eminent maker. Invented the lever escapement in 1757. Entered into partnership with William Dutton in 1755 CC 1738 Plate 52
McCABE, JAMES, London (Royal Exchange & Cheapside). Warden CC. Died 1811. A very good maker. CC 1781 Plates 142 & 98
NORTON, EARDLEY, London. Apprenticed 1762. A famous maker. CC 1770-1794 Plate 93
NOWE, HENRY, London. Recorded as working between 1582 & 1613 Plate 17
PARKINSON & FRODSHAM, London. 1800-1850 Plate 103
PAYNE, JOHN, Lenham. Born 1731 Recorded as working until 1795 Plate 53
PEYTON, RICHARD, Gloucester. Recorded as working before 1740. Died 1774 Plate 51
PERCIVAL, THOMAS, London. 1790-1808 Plate 85
PHILLIPS, JOSEPH, Bristol. Circa 1720-1770 Plates 107 & 108
PICHART, B., Paris. Middle of 17th Century Plate 15
POISSON, HENRY, London. Circa 1695-1720 Plate 33
PRATT, West Hampton. Circa 1760 Plate 106
PURVIS, ALEXANDER, London. Early 19th Century Plate 95
QUARE, DANIEL, London. Born 1649 Master CC 1708 Died 1724. A very famous maker. CC 1671 Plate 38
RAINSFORD, FRANCIS, London. Apprenticed 1681 CC 1689-1709 Plate 30
RAMSAY, DAVID, Dundee, France & London. Arrived in London 1610. Appointed clockmaker to James I in 1613 & was the first Master of the Clockmakers' Co. in 1632. Plate 16
ROOKSBY, JOHN, York. Working in York in 1647 & moved to Hull before 1691. Plate 61
SEDDON, D., Frodsham. Circa 1760 probably a relative of John Seddon who is recorded as working from 1784-1795 Plate 54
SELWOOD, WILLIAM, London. CC 1633-52 Plate 2
SCAFE, WILLIAM, London (King St. Guildhall). Master CC 1749-1764. A noted maker CC 1721 Plates 88 & 89
SORLEY R. & W., Glasgow. Mid 19th Century Plate 122
TOMPION, THOMAS, London 'at the Dial & Three Crowns'. The most famous English maker. Born 1638. Brother of the clockmakers' Company 1671. Assistant 1691, Warden 1700. Master in 1704. Died 1713 Buried in Westminster Abbey. CC 1674 Plates 37, 40 & 43, 68
TURNER, WILLIAM, London. Circa 1785 Plate 52
ULRICH, JOHN, London. Working Circa 1832. Plate 58
VALLIN, NICOLAS, London. Working 1598-1640 Plate 18
VOISIN, ANTOINE H., Paris. 1755-1789 Plate 114
VULLIAMY, B., London. Apprenticed 1775 Clockmaker to George III CC 1781-1820 Plate 111
WAGNER, MICHAEL, Breslav. Recorded as working in the late 17th Century. Died 1704 Plate 11
WALKER, JOHN, London (South Moulton St.). Circa 1880 to present day. Plate 110
WEBSTER, WILLIAM, London (Exchange Alley). Apprentice & journeyman to Thomas Tompion. Warden CC Died 1734. A noted maker CC 1710 Plate 42
WEBSTER, WILLIAM, London (Exchange Alley). Apprenticed 1727 Master 1755 Son of William Webster. An eminent maker CC 1734 Plate 49
WHEELER, THOMAS, London 'near Ye French Church'. Apprenticed in 1647 CC 1655 Master 1684. Died 1694 Plate 19 & 20
WIMBLE, JOHN, Ashford, Kent. Circa 1700-1720 Plate 45
WINDMILLS, JOSEPH, London (Tower St.). Master CC 1702-1723. A very fine maker CC 1671 Plate 41
WINDMILLS, THOMAS, London (Tower St.). Apprenticed 1686 Master CC 1719-1732 Son of Joseph, succeeded to his business. CC 1695 Plate 46

The abbreviation, CC denotes the date when the freedom of the clockmakers' company was granted.

Clock and watch collections

England

Bury St Edmunds:
Gershom-Parkington Memorial
Collection of Time Measurement
Instruments, Angel Corner,
Bury St Edmunds

Cambridge:
Fitzwilliam Museum, Trumpington St.,
Cambridge CB2 1RB

Lincoln:
Usher Gallery, Lindum Rd., Lincoln

Liverpool:
City of Liverpool Museum,
William Brown St.,
Liverpool L3 8EN

London:
British Museum, Great Russell St.,
WC1B 3DG
Clockmakers' Company Museum,
The Guildhall, EC2
National Maritime Museum,
Greenwich, SE10
Science Museum, Exhibition Road,
South Kensington, SW7
Victoria and Albert Museum,
South Kensington, SW7

Oxford:
Ashmolean Museum of Art and
Archaeology, Beaumont St., Oxford
Museum of the History of Science,
Broad St., Oxford, OX1 3AZ

Austria

Vienna:
Clock Museum
Kunsthistorisches Museum

Denmark

Aarhus:
Danish Urmuseum

Copenhagen:
National Museum
Rosenborg Castle Museum

France

Besancon:
Musee des Beaux Arts

Paris:
Conservatoire des Arts et Metiers
Louvre
Musee des Arts Decoratifs

Toulouse:
Musee Paul Dupuy
Musee Saint Raymond

Germany

Augsburg:
City Museum

Baden Wurttemberg:
Collection Landesgewerbeamt

Furtwangen:
Clock Museum

Munich:
Bavarian National Museum

Nuremburg:
Germanisches National Museum

Schwenningen:
Collections of the Mauthe and Kienzle
Factories

Holland

Amsterdam:
Rijksmuseum

Groningen:
Groningen Museum

Leiden:
Dutch Science Museum

Utrecht:
Netherlands Gold, Silver and Clock
Museum

Sweden

Stockholm:
Nordliches Museum
Stadsmuseum

Switzerland

Basel:
Kirchgarten Museum

Geneva:
Musee d'Horologerie

La Chaux de Fonds:
Musee d'Horologerie

Le Locle:
Musee d'Horologerie

Neuchatel:
Musee Historique

USA

CALIFORNIA
San Francisco:
California Academy of Sciences,
Golden Gate Park,
San Francisco, 94118

COLORADO
Denver:
Hagans Clock Manor Museum,
Bergen Park, Evergreen, Denver, 80439

CONNECTICUT
Bristol:
American Clock and Watch Museum,
Inc, 100 Maple St., Bristol, 06010

ILLINOIS
Chicago:
Adler Planetarium and Astronomical Museum,
1300 S. Lakeshore Drive, Chicago, 60605

Springfield:
Illinois State Museum, Spring and Edwards Sts.,
Springfield 62706

MASSACHUSETTS
Sturbridge:
Old Sturbridge Village, Sturbridge, 01566

NEW YORK
New York:
James Arthur Collection, New York University,
Washington Square
Metropolitan Museum of Art, Fifth Ave. at
82nd St., 10028

OHIO
Cincinnati:
Taft Museum, 316 Pike St., 45202

PENNSYLVANIA
Columbia:
National Association of Watch and Clock
Collectors,
514 Poplar St., 17512

VERMONT
Shelburne:
Shelburne Museum, Shelburne, 05482

WASHINGTON D.C.
Smithsonian Institution, 1000 Jefferson Drive,
S.W., 20560

Bibliography

BAILEY, C.H. *Two Hundred Years of American Clocks and Watches,* New Jersey, USA 1976.

BAILLIE, G.H. *Watchmakers and Clockmakers of the World.* London, N.A.G. Press. (Volume II of this book by Brian Loomes adds a further 35,000 names to the list of makers, making a total of over 70,000 clockmakers world wide, and the two volumes are an indispensable reference book for collectors and dealers alike.)

BAILLIE, G.H. *Britten's Old Clocks and Watches and their Makers,* London, 1956.

BASSERMAN, JORDAN *The Book of Old Clocks and Watches,* Allen and Unwin, 1964.

BATTISON, EDWIN, A. and KANE PATRICIA, E. *The American Clock 1725-1865,* Greenwich, Conn, New York Graphic Society Ltd., 1973.

BIRD, A. *English House Clocks, 1600-1850,* Newton Abbott (Devon), 1973.

BRITTEN, F.J. *Watch and Clockmaker's Handbook,* 15th Edition. London, 1955.

BRUTON, E. *Antique Clocks and Clock Collecting,* London, 1974.

BRUTON, E. *Clocks and Watches,* London, 1968.

BRUTON, E. *Dictionary of Clocks and Watches,* London, 1962.

BRUTON, E. *The Longcase Clock,* London, 1976.

CARLE, D. DE *Clocks and Their Value,* London, 1975.

CARLE, D. DE *Practical Clock Repairing,* London, 1971.

CARLE, D. DE *Watch and Clock Encyclopaedia,* London, 1975.

CESZINSKY, H. *Old English Master Clockmakers,* London, 1938.

CESZINSKI, H. nd WEBSTER, M.R. *English Domestic Clocks,* London, 1913. (Reprinted by the Antique Collectors Club, 1976.)

CUMHALL, P.G. *Investing in Clocks and Watches,* London, 1967.

DRUMMOND, ROBERTSON *The Evolution of Clockwork,* S.R. Publishers Ltd., 1931.

EDEY, WINTHROP *French Clocks,* Studio Vista, 1967.

EDWARDES, E.L. *The Grandfather Clock,* Altrincham, 1952.

GAZELEY, W.J. *Watch and Clock Escapements,* London, 1973.

GORDON, G.F.C. *Clockmaking Past and Present* London, 1940.

HAGGAR, A.L. and MILLER, L.F. *Suffolk Clocks and Clockmakers,* Antiquarian Horological Society, 1974.

HOOPES, PENROSE, R. *Connecticut Clockmakers of the Eighteenth Century,* Reprinted 1974, Dover.

JEROME, CHAUNCEY *History of the American Clock Business for the Past Sixty Years,* New Haven: F. C. Drayton, 1860. (Reprinted by Adams Brown, Co., Exeter, New Hampshire)

JORDON, E.V.B. and BERTELE, H. *The Book of Old Clocks and Watches,* (English Edition) London, 1964.

LEE, R.A. *The Knibb Family of Clockmakers,* Byfleet, Surrey, 1964.

LLOYD, H.A. *Chats on Old Clocks,* London, 1951.

LLOYD, H.A. *The Collector's Dictionary of Clocks,* Country Life, 1964.

LOOMES, B. *Watchmakers and Clockmakers of the World,* Vol. II, (see Baillie), London, 1976.

LOOMES, B. *Country Clocks and Their London Origins* Newton Abbott, Devon, 1976.

LOOMES, B. *The White Dial Clock,* Newton Abbott, 1974.

PALMER, BROOKS *The Book of American Clocks,* Macmillan, 1972.

ROBERTS, KENNETH D. *The Contribution of Joseph Ives to Connecticut Clock Technology 1810-1862,* The American Clock and Watch Museum, 1970.

ROBERTS, KENNETH D. *Eli Terry and the Connecticut Shelf Clock,* Ken Robert Publishing Co., 1973.

SYMONDS, R.W. *A Book of English Clocks,* Penguin, 1947.

SYMONDS, R.W. *Thomas Tompion: His Life and Work,* London, 1951.

TYLER, E.J. *European Clocks,* Ward Lock, 1968.

ULLYETT, K. *In Quest of Clocks,* London, 1950.

WARD, F.A.B. *Time Measurement,* A.M.S.O. 1966.

Index

Acknowledgements

The Author and Publishers wish to express their gratitude to the following for their assistance with the illustrations. All photography by David Bassil and Neil Sutherland of Colour Library International Ltd. except where otherwise stated.
Courtesy of the Dean and Chapter, Canterbury Cathedral — Plate 5
Kent Clock Services, Tonbridge — Plate 4
John Carlton-Smith, Imperial Antiques, Chislehurst — Plates 2, 31, 27, 28, 29, 30, 41, 49, 52, 53, 64, 65, 67, 68, 75, 76, 77, 80, 84, 85, 86, 87, 88, 89, 90, 91, 92, 94, 97, 103, 109, 134, 136, 137, 138, 139, 140, 141, 151, 157, 158
Partridge (Fine Arts) Ltd. London — Plates 72, 73, 74, 75, 111, 113, 114, 115, 116, 117
Victoria & Albert Museum, London — Plates 1, 7, 8, 10, 11, 12, 13, 14, 15, 16, 19, 20, 21, 22, 23, 26, 33, 34, 39, 44, 46, 51, 62, 64, 68, 70
Great Brampton House Antiques, Hereford — Plates 3, 96, 111, 119, 122, 123, 130, 132
British Museum — Plates 18, 22, 24, 32, 37, 38, 42, 44, 60, 61, 121 (Supplied by the trustees)
Aspreys, London — Plates 79, 83, 121, 129, 133, 152, 153, 154, 150
Derek Roberts Antiques, Tonbridge — Plates 29, 30, 31, 48, 58, 61, 81, 104, 106, 107, 108, 127, 128
Kingston Antiques, Kingston — Plates 34, 30, 56, 58, 66, 105, 125, 126, 135
Michael Pearson Antiques — Plates 27, 28, 29, 30, 35, 36, 40, 45, 54, 56, 98, 99, 100, 101, 125, 110
Keith Banham Antiques — Plates 93, 142, 147, 151